SWORDS IN THE HANDS OF CHILDREN

Swords in the Hands of Children

Reflections of an American Revolutionary

Jonathan Lerner

OR Books
New York · London

Published for the book trade by OR Books in partnership with Counterpoint Press. Distributed to the trade by Publishers Group West.

All rights information: rights@orbooks.com

First printing 2017

Cataloging-in-Publication data is available from the Library of Congress. A catalog record for this book is available from the British Library.

ISBN 978-1-944869-47-2

Text design by Under|Over. Typeset by AarkMany Media, Chennai, India.

10 9 8 7 6 5 4 3 2 1

I.

A July afternoon at the Chesapeake shore. My husband Peter's family has gathered to celebrate his mother's eighty-fifth birthday. The day is sticky and still, though there's thunder in the distance. We can't swim in the bay because it's alive with stinging jellyfish. Everybody else has taken refuge in the air-conditioned house. I cannonball into the pool, smashing its glassy surface. I'm no diver, and not much of a swimmer. Water explodes around me, slops onto the hot concrete decking, in displacement. For every action, there is an equal and opposite reaction. My body's weight, or mass, or velocity, or all three—I'm not much at physics, either—provoked this agitation. What was tranquil is roiled. I climb out dripping. The ripples die back. Out on the bay now, beyond the sandbar that protects this inlet, I see that a wind has begun kicking up whitecaps.

It has been a turbulent July altogether, this July of 2016. New storms keep whirling me back half a century. I thought I had long since finished brooding over what I did then, and the choices I made, when I called myself a revolutionary. But events of today are forcing me to probe that history one more time. These torments keep coming, like electrical discharges from an angry atmosphere. Yesterday, Miami: a black therapist, trying to manage his autistic patient, shot by police while lying on his back, hands up in surrender. Today, Munich: nine shoppers at a mall; this shooter evidently lacked ideology and was simply crazy, though it's been hard to tell the difference in the recent massacres that inspired him. In Somerville, Massachusetts, the police union demands that a #BlackLivesMatter banner be removed from City Hall; they are reacting to the fact that black snipers have picked off cops in Dallas and Baton Rouge, in retaliation for cops killing black men in Baton Rouge and Minnesota.

Have you lost track of these particular instances of reverberation, cause and effect, among the many deadly interrelated events before and since? No matter. Memory is selective and unreliable. But here's what I'm saying: The Third Law of Motion doesn't apply. Provocations, outrages, postures, slogans, marches, sticks and stones, mass arrests, legally carried assault rifles, deaths, murders. Onward and upward. This chain of actions and reactions, which are oppositional but rarely equal, does not bring things into balance. Tit for tat is perhaps the law in physics, but not, it appears, among human beings. These actions and reactions do not settle back into equipoise, like the surface of the pool, or to any kind of poise. Instead we have backlash and repercussion. Unintended consequences and deliberate consequences. Inflammation and escalation. I am frightened of escalation. I remember how it seduces and blinds. I remember how to incite it. I remember that I once believed there was nothing left for us to do but make things worse. On purpose.

I am sixty-eight this year. I was twenty in 1968, a year of such cascading disaster that it felt to many people, including me, that there could be no rescuing the broken promises of American democracy. That was the bloodiest year of the Vietnam War, a year when more than 43,000 American and allied (South Vietnamese, Thai, Korean, Australian, and New Zealand) soldiers died, along with an estimated 180,000 of their Viet Cong and North Vietnamese enemy combatants, plus uncountable thousands of civilians. It was the year when the police first beat demonstrating American college students bloody on their campuses, and first shot demonstrating American college students dead—black students, they were, in South Carolina. Martin Luther King, Jr., was assassinated, and the angrier voices of black separatism and militance were now eclipsing his non-violent and moral approach to redressing racial inequality. Robert Kennedy, who as president might have tried to end the war, was also murdered; the Democratic mayor of Chicago set his police loose on antiwar demonstrators at the party's convention; and the Democrats lost the election to Richard Nixon, whose racist campaign for "states' rights" and "law and order" prompted a political realignment and polarization that still cripples the country today.

1968 is often considered the pivotal year of the Sixties, "the Sixties" being shorthand here for that era's radical political and cultural upheavals. I use it in this sense to encompass the civil rights movement, the antiwar movement, the Native American sovereignty movement, student power, black power, Chicano power, farmworkers' rights, women's liberation, gay liberation, the back-to-the-land and environmental movements—the multiple upwellings in the United States that arose against a global backdrop of anti-colonial and leftist uprising. The Sixties brought forth real and precious changes, however imperfect and incomplete, openings and shifts in consciousness and culture as well as in law. Among these were also efforts and organizations devoted to militance and to revolution. These too bore fruits, but mostly stunted and rotten fruits, as I know from having tilled that poisoned garden myself.

But the Sixties in this sense was not an exact decade. My own Sixties—my total immersion in activism—began roughly in 1967, when I dropped out of college and joined the staff of Students for a Democratic Society, a big, chaotic but fecund, broadly leftist but relatively welcoming and sometimes even effective mass organization. And for me the pivotal year was not 1968, but 1969. That was when I helped destroy SDS, and from the debris helped found a tiny, secretive, intellectually stultifying, corrupt, and violent revolutionary group called the Weathermen. Soon after its formation, the group became a clandestine organization restyled the Weather Underground. My Sixties—my immersion in the Weathermen— continued until 1976 when the underground began breaking apart. That was a decade, more or less, though one out of sync with the calendar. I was out of sync with a lot in those years, despite, or I should say because of, being in the middle of so much radical furor.

I hadn't set out to tear things apart. My original impulse had been innocent and idealistic. I wanted to humanize the world. My first political act was much earlier, in the summer of 1961, when I was thirteen. I joined a picket line, part of a campaign to desegregate McLean Gardens, an apartment complex in Washington, D.C. This was only a couple of miles from where my family lived in Chevy Chase. I put on a clean shirt and took the bus alone down Wisconsin Avenue, as I had done scores of times before, and hopped off there.

I knew about that demonstration because I'd heard that a group of kids from school I was getting to know, and wanted to be friends with, would be there. To me they were the cool kids, cool because were arty and literary and had ironic senses of humor, and because they went to civil rights events and listened to folk music. So a specific personal impulse—the desire for friendship and belonging—was coexistent with the political. I have come to realize that this was true for me throughout my Sixties. None of those kids showed up that evening at McLean Gardens. But I did become part of their circle, and over the next years we did such things together—white kids knocking on doors in our affluent suburb to collect canned food for the colored people of Greenwood, Mississippi, who were boycotting white businesses; white suburban kids going into Washington's black downtown to the Howard Theater to see the Motown Review, and to a club called the Bohemian Caverns to hear the Modern Jazz Quartet; and skipping school to wander through the National Gallery or to picket in front of the White House during the week between the bloody Selma march and the one that reached Montgomery and the steps of the Alabama State House. We meant all this seriously, and we had a lot of fun doing it. Later, activities I engaged in would be far more serious, and a lot less pleasurable.

McLean Gardens was an unremarkable landmark to me, more or less in the neighborhood where I grew up, just a place we glimpsed in peripheral vision while on the way downtown. That's why, I think now, I took a rather proprietary offense when

I learned it maintained a policy of racial discrimination. No doubt I felt some version of possessiveness, or what we now disparage as entitlement, toward this part of the city. I certainly felt a sense of safety in that comfortable and orderly place, immunity even, so it required no particular courage for me to attend this demonstration.

It wouldn't have occurred to me that there might be any kind of frightening confrontation there. And there wasn't one, given that this was D.C., not Alabama, and it was 1961, when nonviolence and moral suasion were still the tactical essentials of civil rights activism. These twenty or thirty neatly dressed, mainly Negro citizens were not committing civil disobedience but only holding signs and walking in a polite loop, not blocking anyone's way. I don't remember there even being a beat cop in attendance. If there was, I wouldn't have felt threatened. I was at home, secure, white, and privileged; later I lost confidence in this adage, but as I had learned in elementary school, The Policeman was still My Pal. We disparage entitlement rightly enough in its arrogant current manifestations, but perhaps I wouldn't have joined that picket line at all, at thirteen, if I hadn't had the notion that a wrong was being perpetrated in a place where I belonged, and the corollary idea that I had a responsibility—and an ability—to help make it right. It's true that I was nervous that evening, but only because I was the youngest person there. And I didn't know anybody else. Also, I was one of only a handful of white people, and being in favor of civil rights for black people didn't mean I actually knew any black people, aside from the woman who cleaned our house. I didn't know those freedom songs, either. Not yet.

Joining the picket line was a political act, but I didn't see it that way at the time. I didn't yet understand that politics is the exercise of power, a process of struggle, manipulation and maneuvering, bluffing and brinksmanship, noxious sausage making, or even, at best, the art of the possible. I didn't know enough to be scared. My impulse was simply moral. I must have had morality on my mind. My bar mitzvah had been just a month or two earlier. My family was culturally Jewish, if rather indifferently observant. My parents had been founders of one of the first synagogues in Washington's suburbs. Our continuing involvement at that temple was at least as much social as religious; it provided community more than theology, the principal nexus of our circle of family friends.

Unlike many Jews of their generation, these people had not flirted with communism. Most of their parents were Yiddish-speaking immigrants, but they had become professionals and businesspeople, assimilated and successful participants in the postwar American Dream. They were liberals. They believed in American opportunities. They also had the Holocaust seared into their consciousness, which made them compassionate about race. I don't think my parents ever went on any demonstration, but they were among the 75,000 who attended the 1939 concert by the contralto Marian Anderson, performed at the Lincoln Memorial after the Daughters of the American Revolution refused the use of their auditorium because she was Negro. It was the right thing to do. I imagine them feeling proud there. And also enjoying the music.

Preparing for bar mitzvah involved addressing questions and principles of right action in the world. And to be culturally Jewish, as that culture was transmitted to me, is to be aware of and willing to further a tradition of social engagement. Less abstractly, I was inspired by a couple of books I read that summer of McLean Gardens, while sprawled on our shady front porch, which had been bar mitzvah gifts. One was an autographed copy of *Profiles in Courage* by John F. Kennedy, the recently inaugurated President who exuded an idealism I wouldn't have thought to question. The other was *Exodus* by Leon Uris, a gripping saga of Holocaust survival and the birth of Israel, the middlebrow literary quality of which I didn't know enough to impugn.

If picketing at McLean Gardens, whether I thought of it that way or not, was my first political act, it wasn't my first morally inspired gesture. My father was a Foreign Service Officer. Earlier, we had lived in Taipei for two years, 1957 to 1959. This was long before Taiwan became rich and modern. Coming from the leafy, hygienic First World environs of Chevy Chase, the cramped, begrimed poverty we encountered was a shock, uncomfortably—but revealingly—framed by the fact that we lived far more luxuriously there than we ever had at home, within a walled garden, with servants domiciled in a wing off the kitchen that we rarely entered. In 1958 *The Ugly American*, a novel depicting the insensitivity and arrogance of U.S. diplomats in an imaginary Asian country, was causing a sensation in Taipei's American community. I read it then, too.

The ugly American, the physically unattractive character, that is, wasn't a boorish Embassy official isolated among the elite in the capital city, but an unglamorous guy who lived among villagers and did something useful by inventing a bicycle-powered water pump. My mother had joined a committee supporting a desperately impoverished orphanage. I visited there with her and saw scabby, listless children lying two to a cot. I was incensed. And inspired, by that book. So I raised funds from my American pals with which to buy American candy, at the U.S. Navy Commissary, to distribute to these Taiwanese orphans. This is an embarrassing anecdote to relate, revealing as it is of my naïveté, despite the purity of my intentions and the facts that I was only ten years old and that surely those kids enjoyed the sweets.

It is however less embarrassing than recalling that I also devised the winning entry in a Halloween costume contest for children of the Taipei expat community. I dressed as a coolie: barefoot, torn shorts and t-shirt, conical straw hat, a bamboo carrying pole across my shoulders with a cargo basket hung from each end. To us, "coolie" was simply a job description, like cook, driver, or dressmaker, meaning laborer, and coolies, thus attired, were a common sight on Taipei's unpaved streets. I wasn't really that imaginative, I was just copying them.

Later, of course, when I had declared myself an anti-imperialist and revolutionary, the memory of this impersonation—or as it might be called now, appropriation—was mortifying. By then—1969—my father was at the American Embassy in Brazil, where a monstrous military government was torturing and "disappearing" leftist radicals no more radical than I. With glee, I would denounce my father to my comrades as a tool of Amerikkkan global hegemony. We all knew we benefited from being young, white, educated, and more or less affluent, and we ardently flagellated ourselves for it. But hardly any of the others could sketch quite so incriminating a cartoon of their own families' culpability. Perversely, I thought it gave me extra cachet.

When my father retired and he and my stepmother were clearing out of the house in Chevy Chase, a cringeworthy photograph was unearthed of me in that coolie costume. I am posed on the terrace of the Grand Hotel, Taipei's most glamorous venue at the time, where the costume contest was held, high on a cool hillside above the teeming city. By now, though, the image has lost its sting. I was just a kid with some glimmering awareness of the world, and the occasional small impulse to heal it—and good instincts for imagery and presentation. I hadn't set out to tear things apart. I wanted to humanize the world. So how did I end up making so many rash and destructive choices?

• • •

Leave aside my short-lived candy-to-orphans campaign, with its possibly cloying sweetness. It was prompted by genuine feeling, but it wasn't political because it didn't address power, nor did it arise from or contribute to a movement. Consider instead the arc of political and confrontational energy, which was also emotion-driven, that I traveled from 1961 and that decorous picket line at McLean Gardens, through many civil rights events I participated in during my high school years, to 1967 when I was a second-year student at Antioch College in Ohio, and an act of political agitation calculated to provoke, which I helped orchestrate.

A "Spring Mobilization" against the war in Vietnam had been called, for April 15, 1967. The idea was to attract people from across the country to attend massive demonstrations in New York and San Francisco. The war had been steadily intensifying—by that year there were nearly half a million U.S. troops in Vietnam.

Images of the carnage were beamed back daily for the evening news. Among the most appalling were those of Buddhist monks and nuns who protested the war by sitting down in public places, saturating their clothing with flammable liquids, and lighting themselves on fire. I do hope that in doing so they found some kind of transcendence. To their witnesses, these gestures were horrifying, as they surely were meant to be. They were also depressing, expressions of anguish at the inability on the parts of these holy people or anyone else, including people like me and my generation of increasingly engaged American students, to even slow down the war. They were also electrifying in their graphic power. We wanted to prompt Antiochians to go to New York for the mobilization. So we simulated a martyrdom by self-immolation.

It was planned in complete secrecy, to maximize its impact. We did it at dusk, when we knew that virtually all of Antioch's small student body would be in the cafeteria, which had a wall of windows overlooking the street. A VW microbus pulled up in front, with its cargo doors facing away from the building. Cars pulled across the street at both corners to block other traffic. A lifelike dummy, built from a store mannequin, seated in the lotus position, was set onto the street, doused, and lit aflame. All this took mere seconds. As the microbus pulled away, revealing the burning figure, a student, who along with her boyfriend was prominent on campus as an activist, ran into the dining hall screaming, "Dick's set himself on fire!" People raced to the windows, then out to the street. Such a turn of events seemed plausible at that time. Distress about the war was intense. New horrors, and new levels of resistance, seemed to materialize every day. It wasn't uncommon for jailed American antiwar activists to stage hunger strikes. Monks and nuns were burning themselves up over there in the streets of Saigon and Danang. Dick was a locally prominent politico. The dummy looked real. For a while people stood transfixed, believing their eyes.

But unlike a human, the dummy didn't writhe and collapse as it burned. Or groan. Or sizzle. It quickly enough became clear that this was something else: the kind of intervention that was called guerrilla theater then, except by those conversant with the Soviet-Communist tradition who might have termed it agitprop; these days it might be considered performance art. The burning figure wasn't real but the rapid surge and slump of emotion it evoked was real. Now people were enervated, their feelings rawly exposed. The action had been symbolic, and entirely visual—it required no banners or speeches—but nobody watching needed to ask what was being represented. An unplanned element only enhanced the drama, when the campus fire brigade arrived with their hoses. Instead of dispersing as asked, thirty or forty of the spectators joined hands in a silent circle around the fire, some actually weeping—and a few, including me, yelling epithets like "fascist" at the fire brigade—as the thing died down to embers, and darkness came on.

This bit of theater had the desired effect of generating buzz about the war and the mobilization. The next issue of the college weekly was full of it. I had thought of what we did as a *cri de coeur*, a testament, something like Picasso's *Guernica*. I think I had foolishly expected that every person's feelings would mirror mine, so I was surprised to discover that not everyone had been moved to empathy, let alone action. Some people felt attacked, and angry—at us, not at what we called the war machine. The argument seemed ludicrous: We had no right to disrupt the dinner hour with something so unpleasant. I am not sure that anyone actually put it that simplistically; if I misheard at the time, deliberately, or misremember now, then I concede that it belittles our critics to reduce their opinions to the proclamation of a breach of etiquette. Maybe those who didn't like our action had something more nuanced to contribute. Maybe they wanted dialogue.

I still think this action was brilliant, for its clarity and punch. Property damage was limited to a scorch on the asphalt. Nobody was physically hurt, although many were shocked and upset. I said it was calculated to provoke; emotional reaction was the deliberate goal. Shock is one way to get through to people. Grief often accompanies new awareness of a great wrong—conversely, anger can accompany its denial. It sometimes takes a shock to move people to action. We had not provoked a confrontation with any entity of officialdom—excepting the fire brigade, who grumbled, but were merely other powerless students like ourselves. Our intended audience—our target—was not in this case the warmongering government; we were trying to affect our peers, not the country's policies.

Nowadays, doing something like this on the campus of a liberal arts college might be found objectionable for not being preceded by a trigger warning. Of course, its success was based on surprise and the manipulation of sensitivities, as is all effective theater. Regarding our rude despoliation of dinnertime, my feelings today are more convoluted. I quite value my domestic routines now, dinner being an important one in my daily scheme of things. Usually I have cooked it, and gone to some effort. Peter and I use cloth napkins. We often light candles, put on relaxing music. I make a point of not looking at my phone while I'm at the table, on the theory that nothing could be so urgent that it can't wait a few minutes, and that the benefit of an uninterrupted meal with my husband surpasses that of any instantaneously delivered particle of new information. More generally, I ration my intake of current events. And pretty much the only social media I pay attention to is a Facebook community page for the small city where we live, on which announcements of yard sales, lost cats, and road closures dominate. These are protective tactics I have settled on to keep myself sane in an assaultive world. I may be less resilient than I was when young, or even less open-minded, or maybe I'm just less hungry for a constant feed of outrages, since I've long ago learned that when it can't get any worse, it will. I'm certainly less reactive, by which I mean less hotheaded—and definitely less hungry for a fight. I am almost always aware that my energy is finite. I practice conservation.

I could argue that things were different then, because of that horrible war being waged in our name, which demanded a little physically harmless political rudeness for the righteous purpose of waking up the people. But there are wars being waged in our name today. There is the asymmetrical global and evidently permanent one, which America's military might, vacillating foreign policy, and bloated intelligence services seem incapable of getting a handle on. And there is the war at home, under way long centuries before new technology brought it into mass focus, the casualties of which tend to be mainly black men plus just recently, in reaction, and to a great many people's inexplicable surprise, uniformed policemen as well. Just to name two of today's horror shows. So I can't argue against disruptive guerrilla theater, or agitprop, in principle, even as I put considerable effort into defending my own tranquil experience of dinner. If I were to diagram the back and forth and ever-upward escalation of hostilities between the radical movement and the state in the Sixties, our staged faux-suicide at Antioch would hardly figure, or would at most be penciled in so lightly as to be illegible.

But it did contribute to polarization in our small college community. And it did embolden those of us who pulled it off, and others elsewhere who heard about it, and it may well have inspired other guerrilla theatricals. That's another kind of escalation, which is internal, and functions the same within individuals and groups: You do something bold and it has the result you sought, or do something transgressive and get away with it, so the next thing you do is bolder and more transgressive. I could make a separate diagram of the left's escalation of propaganda and of tactics like guerrilla theater during the years that followed; some were considerably less polite than our immolated dummy at dinnertime.

What troubles me about escalation, in the context of artistic gestures in particular but also conflict in general, is the ease with which nuance can get lost, and dialogue discouraged. Yelling "fascist" at the fire guys, for example. That wasn't scripted, it just struck me as the thing to do in the moment. The fire guys actually were the occupants of a dorm called Maples, the closest thing to a fraternity at countercultural Antioch. They might really have been more conservative politically than the rest of the mildly to wildly leftist student body. Some of them, or even most of them, might have been supporters of the war. But since I never spoke to any of them I wouldn't know. Certainly the students in Maples were willing to commit to a kind of community-oriented activity, if not activism, that people like me ridiculed as unfashionably virtuous and square. (My own dorm never caught fire so I never needed the help they volunteered at considerable personal risk.) But if we truly wanted to appeal to our community's powers of reason, or compassion, Maples should have been included. My small impulsive escalation, calling them a repellant name, could hardly have made those guys feel welcome to chat.

What we did that evening in front of the cafeteria wasn't as directly and universally embraced as I had expected. But I didn't dwell on its shortcomings. I was too thrilled at its having been such a well-orchestrated clandestine operation with such a splashy outcome. My first. Not my last.

• • •

That internal kind of escalation: You dare to do something, get away with it, and then dare acts bolder still. Here's an example.

A couple of months after that evening of the burning dummy in Ohio, I was living in New York City where there was a loose community of Antiochians. Some were there on jobs, as part of the college's work-study program. Some, like me by then, had dropped out. In 1967, if you were the sort of kid who dropped out of a sort of college like Antioch, the most likely places to land were San Francisco or New York. I had this vague notion of going into theater—to be a lighting designer, or a stage manager, or even an actor or a dancer—so New York was the natural choice. My Antioch friend Jeff Jones had dropped out and moved to the city around the same time. We were close, although our backgrounds and personalities were different. While I had been picketing McLean Gardens, Jeff had been at Boy Scout camp. But in college, where I mainly paid attention to arts, he embraced radical politics. When he quit school that summer, it was to become a full-time organizer, on the New York staff of SDS.

The next big national antiwar mobilization was a march on the Pentagon, that October, to culminate a week of demonstrations around the country. Jeff suggested that when I got to D.C. for the march, I stop at the SDS staff house there. When I did, the vibe was grim. Street-blocking actions, aimed at shutting down the Armed Forces Induction Center in Oakland, had been attacked by the police. A lot of people there had been hurt and arrested. In Madison, students had tried to deny entry onto the university campus to recruiters from Dow Chemical, manufacturers of napalm, the incendiary chemical being used to defoliate Vietnam's jungles in order to reveal guerrilla hideouts. The Wisconsin students had suffered similar tear-gassing and beatings as their California counterparts.

We'd seen police attack demonstrations before—but at the remove of our television screens—during civil rights demonstrations of mostly black people, in the South. We'd seen, on TV, police hosing and tear-gassing crowds during the riots, the inchoate insurrections that erupted every year in one or more depressed black sections of Northern cities back then. (The media-bestowed name for these recurring seasons of conflagration was "the long hot summer"; I haven't heard it used during this long hot 2016 summer of racial conflict, but perhaps only because I don't watch TV news.) Oakland and Madison were the first times that a demonstration by young, privileged, overwhelmingly white people of our generation had been bloodied. Gathered at the Washington SDS house that night were many of the organization's leaders. They were grappling with how to respond, and how to act during the mobilization that Saturday. A year later I would be living in that Washington SDS house, a staff member myself. At moments like this I would be one of those packed into the smokey, barely furnished living room while other semi-initiated, tentative activist friends and hangers on would be standing around in the hallway and on the stairs, anxious to listen, as I was now.

When Jeff saw that I had arrived, he took me outside. As we walked around the block, he recruited me into a secret, decentralized action for the eve of the big demo. It was another inventive and thrilling example of agitprop, right up my alley. Teams would spray-paint slogans on the sides of city buses. Most buses today are mobile billboards—our underfunded transit systems have to subsidize themselves with advertising—but back then they were simply long, unadorned boxes. Similarly, cities' other blank surfaces had not yet been appropriated by graffiti writers and muralists. Today's graphic urban chaos didn't yet exist. I imagined the visual impact of hundreds of those green D.C. Transit buses chugging through town inadvertently spreading antiwar messages while thousands of us marched on the headquarters of the war machine. Of course I said I'd do it.

The idea was to go out in twos and wait at bus stops. When a bus came, one person would start to board but do something to delay, like asking the driver complicated directions, or hunting through pockets for the right change. Meanwhile the partner would tag the vehicle's long side. Jeff swore me to secrecy. I rounded up another Antioch friend of ours, and we two modified the plan.

I knew an unfenced lot, at the end of a line near my family's house, where dozens of buses were parked overnight. We would be able to hit more of them, faster. We separated to move down the dark aisles between the buses, cans of spray paint blazing away like automatic weapons. Suddenly I had the thought that there might be a watchman. What if one were to come around the end of a row and discover me? It never occurred to me that he might be armed. And given the era's now-unimaginable absence of security, I'm pretty sure a watchman at a bus yard wouldn't have been armed—if there even would have been a watchman. The answer seemed suddenly obvious. It was right in my hand. I would spray him in the face, blind him if I could, and get away with ease. No italics, no exclamation point. It would be easy. I would just do it. "Armed" self-defense in the service of the struggle.

Oh, I thought next, I guess that means I'm not a pacifist. I felt a slight shift in my gut, but the change seemed as barely perceptible as a gland squirting out an enzyme, this escalation of permission, from myself to myself, to slip restraints, shrug off consequences, decouple meaning from action. When the action could mean injuring a person. Had I even been a pacifist? I certainly had never spent any time thinking through the meaning and morality of pacifism. But my idea of activism had been informed by the non-violent ethic of the civil rights movement. I had also witnessed, from a distance, the sacrifices such commitment could extract. I understood the honor pacifism declaims even as it admits to inferior strength: We are weak against your might, but stronger in our souls.

Blind him. I really thought that I would do that. Thinking it made me feel good. I've always avoided conflict. I've never been a fighter. When I was bullied in junior high school, taunted for being a fag, I never struck back physically, or even verbally, though I might compose a silent withering comeback or mutter one to a friend. Now a different stance was revealing itself as available to me. A radically changed me, one with a nervy, devil-may-care, superior bearing.

This new posture went untested that night. No watchman appeared. So I had committed another supposedly daring political act without cost to myself. Maybe there had been no risk, because there was nobody to catch us. Whatever risk there was had been mitigated by our stealth. The secrecy felt good, too.

• • •

Fear was perfectly reasonable when the confrontations were with the police, which most were; the police had the motivation, training, and gear to whip our butts and then throw us in jail. Fear was also reasonable when we got into fights with aggressive civilians, as occasionally happened. I did perhaps over time adopt a strut, and perhaps at times radiate a brashness, even a slight menace. But I was always deeply afraid when it came to a fight. My new easy-come audacity was tested the very next day, revealing itself to be equally easy-go.

The demonstration began with a rally at the Lincoln Memorial and a march across the bridge, where a militant contingent broke through a fence and led a whooping charge across a lawn toward the Pentagon. To our surprise, nothing prevented us from mounting the steps to the terrace at the base of the building. We milled around for a little while—feeling pleased with ourselves but unsure what to do next—when hundreds of soldiers and U.S. Marshals emerged from the building, truncheons dangling from their belts, rifles with fixed bayonets in their arms. They formed a shoulder-to-shoulder wall between the building and us. Now all the elements of a standoff were in place.

By evening, we had settled in, most of us sitting in a large mass. It grew dark and chilly. Some people tried to reason or argue with the soldiers who were looming over them, who were mostly kids like us, of our generation. I wasn't right in front, but maybe twenty feet back in the crowd. From time to time there would be an irresistible provocation from our side, or an implacable need to punish from theirs, and a group of them would push as a wedge into the seated crowd. It was terrifying. You could hear yelling and screaming but not quite see what was going on, until TV crews switched on their lights and swept the crowd, trying to locate the action, their beams strobing off the polished wood of thrashing truncheons. This was the kind of thing you watched on TV, not in the flesh a few feet in front of yourself. It went on all night: uneasy quiet broken by periodic mayhem.

It ended because our side dwindled away. They won tactically; we claimed the moral victory. I was with a bunch of friends from college. We left around dawn. I brought them home to Chevy

Chase. People tried to sleep, took showers, made travel plans, but mostly sat around stupefied. I had not yet thrown myself into the movement, as Jeff had done—though I would very soon. And the night we had just lived through made me realize that physical confrontation would be a fact of life in radical activism. I felt exhausted and, even in the safety of my family's living room, afraid. And felt the correlative of that fear: shame, for feeling afraid.

Fear can be a disincentive to action. Shame, on the other hand, as I came to know well, can be a great motivator.

• • •

Two weeks later I became a member of the SDS staff. This seems a mighty abrupt shift, looking back. I was moderately politically active, in an emotional and instinctive way. But I was not at all ideological. I didn't think about politics strategically, I just responded. I had never thought of myself as an organizer. If I had ever attended an SDS meeting at Antioch, I can't recall it. But I definitely had never been a member of the organization. Of course, I wasn't oblivious to political conditions in the world.

The Vietnam War was an ever-intensifying drip-drip on the forehead. The war in Vietnam was vividly in our faces in ways that our wars in Afghanistan and Iraq have not been. Press coverage was not managed then as it is now. We saw new footage every day of battles and carnage, crashed helicopters and burning villages. The Pentagon issued a daily body count; they manipulated the numbers, but futilely, because it still kept the blood and destruction on our minds. Vietnam affected people my age in a particular way: Every boy between eighteen and twenty-five was vulnerable to being drafted into the military. The boys were confronted with the possibility of being sent to fight, while the girls were confronted with a system that wouldn't have allowed them to fight if they wanted to. Even if you had a student or medical deferment, you knew people who were headed for Nam. I myself had been called up for induction, and only by saying I was homosexual did I guarantee my rejection. Escaping the possibility of finding myself in Vietnam was an enormous relief, though in those days admitting to being gay was an enormous humiliation. Coming out, even in cosmopolitan New York, demanded courage I didn't have; I was still far from accepting myself as gay.

On civil rights, progress seemed agonizingly slow. Little seemed improved in conditions of life for most black people. Groups advocating militance and black separatism were beginning to splinter away from the non-violent mainstream movement, which had focused on integration. Racial tensions were high. Living in New York in that summer of 1967 it would have taken deliberate effort, for example, to ignore the six days of rioting that paralyzed Newark, across the river. The conflict broke out after white cops arrested and beat up a black cab driver, following which a rumor started that he died in custody. *Plus ça change.*

I also knew there were radical movements elsewhere, anticolonial uprisings in the Third World, leftist student movements akin to ours in Western Europe and Latin America and Japan. I knew about it when Che Guevara, already an international icon of rebellion, was captured and killed just a few weeks before the Pentagon demonstration while he was trying to create a revolutionary army in rural Bolivia. I knew these things the way millions of people who did not define themselves as activists knew these things, people whose activism was just something they did in addition to being a student or a mother or a cab driver or a stoned hippie. I couldn't escape knowing, and I didn't want to, even though knowing, and contemplating a response, made me afraid.

In the five months since I'd arrived in the city I had taken a few acting and dance classes. I performed in a couple of obscure workshop productions. I briefly had a part-time job in a toy store, from which I was fired because friends would stop in to hang out with me too often. Then I found a part-time job collating survey data at an ad agency. Occasionally I worked as an artist's model. But I felt an unsettling disconnect between what I was doing with my time and my impulse to respond to political reality. So to my patched-together weekly schedule I added participation in a political street theater. We went around to parks to act out didactic skits about the war and distribute flyers announcing upcoming demonstrations. All this made a rickety scaffolding to support a life on my own in the big city. If I had any real aptitude for theater I wasn't going to cultivate it in this haphazard way, and I certainly lacked the drive a theater career demands, never mind appropriate talent. Besides which, the ubiquity and openness of gay people in theater frightened me.

When I first got to New York I crashed with some Antioch pals who were there working as part of the college's work-study program. They went back to school in the fall, and I got my own tiny apartment. Both of these places were in what's now the fashionable East Village, but was then a tense, depressing slum. It had been easy enough to ignore the unpleasantness in the summer;

now I was facing it alone. At nineteen, I was living independently, like a grownup without quite being one. My mother had died three years before. My father was checked out: A complete transcript of his reply to my breezy telephoned announcement that I was dropping out of college would read, "OK." My sister and older brother were both living in New York then, but there was a limit to the support they could give me, and a limit to the concern I was willing to accept because accepting it would imply that I needed it. And I could no longer rely on the naturally occurring community a school environment might provide. Worse, after the Pentagon, whenever I thought about the state of the world, which I could not help doing, I got a wobbly cramp in my gut at the memory of those swinging truncheons, and my fear of them, and my inability to stop them. It was November. The days were getting darker.

Through my friendship with Jeff, I had been getting to know people in the orbit of the New York regional SDS office, but only casually and socially. I shared a few beggars'-banquet dinners with this loose group of friends, a few joints. A bunch of us went to the movies to see *The Battle of Algiers*, which depicts the urban guerrilla campaign that had dislodged France from colonial control of Algeria a few years earlier. We left the theater giddy, high on the impression the film gave—or, the impression we took away—that clandestinity was the key to revolution. Soon after the Pentagon, a couple of Jeff's confederates invited me over and asked me to join the staff.

SDS had a structure, but a vanishing minimal one that stopped well short of defining who could represent and run the organization at the local level. This improvisational, folksy culture was a strength. It made room for many kinds of ideas and degrees of commitment, much creativity and ferment. It was also a weakness, allowing easy infiltration by police agents, and manipulation by ideological factions.

There wasn't any formal hiring or vetting process, just a couple of people who had decided I ought to be on the staff and invited me on board. When I protested that I had nothing to offer, they countered with the flattering proposal that I should organize guerrilla theater groups in the campus chapters. Also I could help run the office, open the mail, answer the phone. I didn't feel a need to think hard about the implications of taking this step—any more than I had thought about the implications of dropping out of college. A snap decision was easy. Joining the SDS staff would give me community, identity, and participation in a bold response to the world. And $15 of "subsistence" per week, when the treasury had any money. It would also place me closer to my pal Jeff. With whom I was, in a constricted and unarticulated way, in love.

You can never know, before you throw yourself into something, quite what being in it will be like. Accepting a job, entering a marriage, joining an organization: You're always taking a chance. Still, you can try in advance to know more, or less. You can choose with caution, or abandon. You can take a step that might reasonably be expected to lead down a path you want to travel, toward the person you want to be and the life you want to have, or you can close your eyes, jump, and mend broken bones later. It is certainly not the case that every person who joins a political organization—who joined SDS or its staff, or even joined Weatherman, later, in the season of pandemonium when that option presented itself—did so with as little objective forethought as I. Just as it is not the case that every member of my generation, or even every Antioch dropout with artsy and leftish sensibilities, had as vague, or nonexistent, a life plan as I. For me, joining the staff filled a void and muzzled some distressing emotions. Suddenly I was a "full-time organizer" or—as I soon called myself, emulating Jeff and others—a "professional revolutionary." Hey, look! I just got a profession, and I didn't even have to finish college! And it was a profession that could make me an actor not in sparsely attended theatricals held in side-street industrial lofts, but on the world stage. It promised, instead of the slim likelihood of a critic's review, massive public triumph—on the glorious day when we would succeed in taking state power. We really thought that would happen.

I needed, or surely could have used, psychotherapy in that fall of 1967. My sister talked me into trying it but I quickly quit, there being that crucial difference between needing and wanting. My idealism and my concern about race relations and the war were authentic. But this step into full-time activism was at least compensatory, and my flirtation with violence was compensatory, too, if not pathological. Joining something to fill a hollow in yourself might coexist with joining to work toward a shared vision, but those aren't the same thing. Of course, once you've joined, it is easy enough to embrace the official vision and memorize the approved rhetoric. Still, there is a great deal of difference between me in 1967 when I joined the SDS staff, or even in 1969 when my Weatherman comrade Teddy Gold and I fantasized about detonating a bomb on a Chicago El train, on one hand, and on the other hand, for example, Omar Mateen. By some accounts a panicked self-loathing homosexual, Mateen murdered dozens of people at a gay bar in Orlando earlier in this hot summer of 2016, justifying himself with a garbled version of Islamic terrorist ideology. I say I needed therapy, but I wasn't anywhere near that crazy. Although I will get around to showing you, from my own experience, how the fear and shame of being gay and seeing no way out of the closet can propel a person to make regrettable choices.

I feel a degree of empathy with the perpetrators of some of the recent, heinous ideologically or politically rationalized terrorist acts. I grew up white and male in affluent Chevy Chase, with a cornucopia of options that extended to dropping out of a good college without pausing to worry about my future. My circumstances had nothing in common with those of someone, like many such actors today, who is recruited or recruits himself to terrorist action after growing up in a dreary ghettoized section of some glittering metropolis such as New York or Paris or London, with little prospect of meaningful work or full acceptance by the dominant culture. But every person who chooses that path toward violence and terrorism has a psychological twist or problem or a complex of them, as did I, and is doing so at least partly to compensate.

Except perhaps in cases like Omar Mateen's where repressed sexuality may be a factor, I have little comment to offer on the specific psychological issues of young people in Western countries who march off to join terrorist armies in the Middle East, or attack their neighbors at home in the name of those armies. They might be overwrought, even clinically diagnosable. But their choices are also fueled by anger and hopelessness that have a basis in reality, just as rage and despair were stirred in me by a system of indefensible wrongs and the seeming inability of heartfelt mass movements to correct them. What drove me in the Sixties may not be equivalent to whatever conditions today might prompt a volunteer jihadi, or an ex–U.S. Army Reservist with excellent sniper skills, to commit an act of terrorism—conditions such as, perhaps, a perceived perpetual war against one's people, or the personal prospect of a lifetime of discrimination, impoverishment, and humiliation. But I can say that rage and despair at real conditions are very likely aswirl in their minds, along with and inextricable from the emotional needs and flaws that let them give themselves permission to act destructively. And I can relate to that willingness to destroy, that feeling of righteousness in lashing out justified by the perception—the misperception—that nothing else will work.

In the United States nowadays, inheriting a bleak present and a dead-end future can motivate people not only to immerse themselves in radical ideologies but also—and far more often, thankfully—to become soldiers or cops. The all-volunteer military we have had since the draft ended is full of kids who come from moribund communities and have had inferior schooling. The service offers a way out, and the promise of skills and education. Law enforcement, similarly, can provide a career in an industry that is not going to shut down or move away. Soldiering and policing are honorable professions. But just like people in thrall to a radical ideology who become unhinged and violent, soldiers and cops possessed of twisted psychology or ideology can also become carelessly, or even deliberately, brutal. Think of Abu Ghraib— the Iraqi prison where in 2003 American soldiers took it upon themselves to invent shameful tortures for detainees, and snapped photos of themselves doing so; or of Abner Louima, the Haitian immigrant who in 1997 was savagely beaten and sodomized with a broom handle by a New York cop who then strutted around the station house bragging about it.

Of course, the military and the police are civic institutions, and unlike clandestine insurgencies or holy-war-waging armies and the lone wolves they inspire, soldiers and cops come by their magnificent ordnance legally. So their leaders and the public officials those leaders answer to—and ultimately we, the public ourselves—are responsible for preventing unhinged bullies from taking on such important and stressful work, and for preventing them from thinking that they have official sanction to go around acting like terrorists.

• • •

I also did it for love.

I joined for the warm social scene, the humane communalism, around the New York SDS office in 1967, the shared money and meals, the easy assumption of friendship, the frequent genuine intimacy. As I got to know the organization I discovered that I was now part of a network of people spread across the country, with whom all this was also assumed, also possible. In larger and more formal gatherings—meetings, rallies—we used a language learned in the civil rights movement, calling each other sisters and brothers. This language can be thrilling on the lips of a gifted orator who is beseeching you to open your heart to the world's people and their pain, and to do something about it. A poster on the office wall bore a quote from Che Guevara—young, bearded, handsome, at once soldierly and starry-eyed, and now freshly martyred; there was not a more romantic figure—"At the risk of seeming ridiculous, let me say that the true revolutionary is guided by a great feeling of love." Later there would come a more elaborate and combative rhetoric of anti-imperialism and internationalism and wannabe communism, and tortuous ideological constructs through which we pledged solidarity with and even obeisance to various movements and rebellions here and abroad, and to tyrannical leaders in countries about which we knew fuck all, such as Enver Hoxha of Albania.

Maybe that kind of screed was already forthcoming in 1967, but if so I didn't notice. The culture of SDS was still informed by the organization's beneficent founding principles and spirit, such as a commitment to participatory democracy, and an early goal of building "an inter-racial movement of the poor." And SDS people could not have helped being infused with the dreamier aspects of the counterculture—"all you need is love," and a tendency toward magical thinking—especially the younger and more pot-addled among us. Dreamily innocent myself, I believed in all this perhaps too literally, and was shocked a few months later when at a regional SDS conference a repellently unlovable Maoist sect called Progressive Labor nearly succeeded at taking control of the New York office. Joylessly disciplined to a 1930s-era vision of industrial workers' revolution, averse to militance in the streets and flamboyance of any kind, which they feared would alienate their precious proletariat, PL seemed like alien spawn. In reaction, we drew closer—we, the cool people, the hip, rock-and-rolling, arty, sexy, loving people. Including Jeff.

I noticed Jeff Jones my first day at Antioch, tossing a frisbee on the lawn between our dorms. He could have been a poster child for the postwar promise of Southern California, having left a '65 Mustang behind in the San Fernando Valley, where he had been president of his high school student council. He was dazzlingly blond. He had a sunny disposition. He surfed. He played frisbee, for god's sake—to me, the essence of square. Meanwhile I was arty, moody, and trying hard to radiate East Coast boho sophistication. We were so divergent in background and character that our nascent friendship felt continually surprising and exotic. He loved the wild, and I credit him for awakening my own appreciation of nature, on long walks in the reserve that adjoins the Antioch campus. Later, during the underground years, when we seldom saw each other, he took care to plan our meetings as hikes around a lake or to a mountain viewpoint.

In 1989, thirteen years after the demise of the Weather Underground, a publisher asked me to write a memoir. Fortunately, it was rejected. For one thing, it lacked focus; I hadn't grasped the considerable difference between memoir and history. Also, I skewed the story through the lens of my sexuality—my impossible infatuations with straight male leader types, hapless attempts at affairs with women, feeble ambivalent gestures toward self-acceptance. Many gay writers feel compelled to tell their coming out tales. Mine is inextricable from this story but not its center; eventually I wrote a novel, *Alex Underground*, that satisfied the impulse.

In the course of researching that unpublished memoir I traveled around to interview old comrades. "I'd still always rather be outdoors," Jeff confirmed when I visited him. "Like, I don't believe there is such a thing as bad weather." He also told me, "You were the person who taught me to read the Sunday *New York Times* from cover to cover while eating bagels and drinking coffee." If I had not made friends with Jeff, I would be writing a different book now. I would have been a radical somehow; that was the inevitable conjunction of my character and the times, though it's quite unlikely that I would have joined the SDS staff, or Weatherman. But here is what actually happened: Jeff was involved at the center of the SDS, and he led me in.

(Regarding nomenclature, I use the name Weatherman and its many variations unconventionally, but as we did at the time. So the organization was Weatherman, or alternately the Weathermen, and later became the Weatherman Underground, and when that began to sound a little male chauvinist, the more gender-neutral Weather Underground. We had Weather collectives comprised of Weatherpeople—Weathermen and Weatherwomen or, generically, Weather cadre—who lived in Weather apartments, and were supported by Weather sympathizers, more derisively called Weathersymps, and so on.)

The camaraderie in SDS that I recall as so cosseting and fulfilling sometimes lacked depth, and was at least partly situational—forced in the hothouse of our belligerent stance toward the state, and by the intensity of the moment. We sometimes made facile assumptions about people, and took risks with them on the basis of sketchy knowledge. If I trust Tom, and Tom is friends with Dick, and Dick is roommates with Harry, and Harry has to split to Canada to dodge the draft, then sure, I'll drive Harry through the night to Montreal in a car belonging to yet another person I don't know. But some connections were genuine and deep. And fifty years on, after the tumult of Weatherman, the ruptures and recriminations when it ended, and the scattering away to separate lives, I still retain from those days one profound friendship, plus a few other real friends whom I don't see much but can pick up with instantly whenever I do. That's something. Jeff, though, is not among them.

• • •

I never personally drove anybody through the night to Montreal to escape the draft. I did occasionally carry out similar tasks, in SDS days, and sometimes with similar nonchalance, although later, in the underground days, I was often cited for my prudence and creativity at what we would come to call "clandestine practice." But from the moment I joined the New York staff I was aware that behind the public rallies and chapter meetings in dormitory common rooms and the nascent sectarian battles, behind the raucous visible bustle, there was another dimension of secret, illegal activity going on.

It was mainly focused on draft resistance, helping boys get themselves rejected by suggesting ruses they could employ or, if those failed and they were still determined, how to acquire landed immigrant status in Canada. Sometimes, more daringly, it involved helping guys who were already in the military to bolt. In the face of the war's stupefying irrationality, this was moral and clearheaded work; I wish more of it had been done, especially aiding deserters, to destabilize the military and hasten the end of the war. I was not myself much involved, but knowing this was going on was thrilling, and reassuring. It suggested seriousness, preparation, a long view; it prefigured an underground as if one were already in place. And this hidden work represented escape, from the relentless escalation of conflict out in the open that felt threatening. Is secret activity as a form of safety unbelievable? For me, that was always part of its allure.

I made maybe three fruitless visits to SDS chapters to promote guerrilla theater endeavors, before abandoning the idea that this would be my work. I spent a lot of time in the office, which was soothingly removed from the confrontations. But there really wasn't any escape from them. In mid-November, within weeks of the Pentagon and my joining the staff, a demonstration outside the Hilton to protest an appearance by the Secretary of State, unlike the standoff at the Pentagon, took on an unstable, fissile, motile quality. The crowd seethed through the streets around the hotel. People blocked traffic, set trash cans alight and rolled them into traffic, threw stones and bottles and eggs at the cops. I attended dressed as a bloodied soldier, with my street theater troupe; we had devised a skit to perform for passersby, but the costumes and make-up just marked us out and got in our way as we ran to escape the police. They charged us on motor scooters and on horseback. Our chants and their sirens echoed down the Midtown canyons. We threw marbles onto the pavement, hoping the horses would stumble. The spectral TV-crew lights flashed jarringly on and off.

I arrived at the office the next day hoping for a numbing few hours filling literature orders. But reporters kept calling, seeking comment. Paul Millman, another Antioch friend less green and more cocky than I, was willing to talk. "It's a hell of a way to live," he shouted into the phone. "And it may be a hell of a way to die. But they're not leaving us any choice."

There wasn't much action in New York in the cold months. But in February of 1968 in tropical Vietnam, the North Vietnamese army and Viet Cong guerrilla forces—the communists—launched their dazzling Tet Offensive. It was a simultaneous surprise attack on over a hundred towns across South Vietnam that even managed to capture, temporarily, the U.S. Embassy in Saigon. It was two weeks before American and South Vietnamese forces once again had control of the capital, and twice that before they could retake the historic imperial, and strategic, city of Hue. Tet was militarily brilliant, revealing the communists' strength and capabilities, but it naturally provoked a fierce escalation in response. It did not result in any quick end to the war, which bled on for another ghastly seven years.

Winter is also mild in South Carolina, where that same month students at the all-black state college in Orangeburg demonstrated to integrate a bowling alley. Police fired on them. Thirty-three were injured, three killed. Did those kids expect that demanding the right to go bowling could get them killed? Live bullets fired at demonstrating American students? This was apocalyptic and new. James Foreman, a veteran leader of non-violent integration efforts in the South who was now on a trajectory toward black separatism and militance, spoke to a gathering I attended. His bitterness was not limited to the perpetrators of Orangeburg, but directed, too, at us, white radicals. You can do anything without risk of being shot, he told us. Now what are you going to do about Orangeburg?

What, indeed?

Jeff and I had moved together into an apartment on the Lower East Side, and pretty soon his new girlfriend Phoebe Hirsch moved in with us. This was awkward, physically and emotionally. It was a typical cramped Old Law tenement apartment with one bedroom, although rather deluxe because instead of a tub in the kitchen and toilet in the hall it had acquired a real bathroom. Jeff and Phoebe had the bedroom and I slept in the living room. It wasn't easy for me to see them so wildly in love, so close up. But Phoebe was another arty, intense East Coast Jewish kid—his type, I guess—and she and I felt immediately familiar to each other and genuinely liked each other, and came to trust each other. Maybe the trust was enhanced the evening I was home alone, getting ready to cook dinner for us all, when she came pounding breathlessly in the door, having raced up the stairs to escape a man who came at her with a knife in the building's entryway, and I helped her calm down. It was a rough neighborhood then.

During that same month of February 1968, there was a strike by New York's sanitation workers. A sharp-witted, tightly wound anarchist and artist named Ben Morea organized an action in which people filled shopping carts with garbage from the fetid piles accumulating on the streets of the Lower East Side. The refuse was dragged uptown and dumped onto the plaza at Lincoln Center, gleaming temple of official high culture. The accompanying leaflet Ben wrote ended with a line adapted from the poet LeRoi Jones, who had not quite yet renamed himself Amiri Baraka and proclaimed his own advocacy of black separatism and armed self-defense: "Up against the wall, motherfucker, and into the trash can."

Ben and friends also staged an action in response to Orangeburg, inside Grand Central Station at rush hour, at which somebody fired off a blank pistol, inducing panic. Jeff told me, when I saw him in 1989, that the first discussion he ever participated in about establishing a secret, armed organization took place at Ben's place around that time. "I was torn, as I always was torn, between politics and mayhem," Jeff recalled. But instead, a loose and very public group was formed—part agitprop commando and part street-fighting squad, which included Jeff, Phoebe, me, and others from SDS—that became known as the Motherfuckers.

One goal of its antics and rants was to taunt SDS toward edgier action. It was a Motherfucker who lobbed a cream pie into the face of the director of the military draft system when he spoke at Columbia University. In late April, in this atmosphere of hit-and-run theater and escalating hostility, the SDS chapter at Columbia led an occupation of five campus buildings—another new scenario, which was to be emulated the following year at scores or maybe hundreds of American colleges. The occupiers included plenty of outside agitators—non-Columbia SDS people, rabble-rousing Motherfuckers, and other unaffiliated radicals hungry for action. After a week, the protest was violently quashed by the police, with 700-plus arrests.

Jeff told me that a few years later he came across a quote from Daniel Cohn-Bendit, the mouthpiece of the massive French student uprising of May '68, saying that it had been inspired by the Columbia strike. "So you see, it all traces right back to the Lower East Side and the Motherfuckers," Jeff said in 1989, in one of his charming signature rhetorical sweeps. Back to us, it seemed he was implying: to New York SDS, or to those SDS militants of 1968 who one year later coalesced into Weatherman. Or maybe back to just him and me. Perhaps his putting it like that was an attempt to curry reconnection. Our previous encounter, when the organization was tearing itself apart in 1976, had been bleak, an ending. He was gracious to let me visit and interview him now. But the thrill was gone.

• • •

SDS was an organization but also a series of events, an endless permutation, an unfurling cloud. Or you could picture it as a Venn diagram in which smaller circles, or irregular shapes, intersected the central one. The center encompassed the campus chapters, offices, "regional travelers" who organized where there was no office, and dues-paying members. Compared to its influence, SDS' actual paid membership was always small, ten, possibly twenty thousand at the peak. But then there were amorphous circles of hundreds and of hundreds of thousands who attended the chapter meetings and teach-ins and joined the marches.

There was the community-organizing-in-poor-urban-neighborhoods circle, a remnant of that early SDS vision of an interracial movement of the poor. There were other circles, distinct organizations really, having nominal affiliation to SDS, like Teachers for a Democratic Society, or simply ones that shared affinities of motivation and world view, like the North American Congress on Latin America, a research group that still exists, or the Newsreel, which made documentary films, or Liberation News Service, which provided content to radical publications. In this last category, in scores of places around the country, were the groups cranking out underground newspapers—"underground" didn't mean they were clandestine, just rebellious in spirit. Also there were several other more tightly disciplined leftist organizations, including Progressive Labor, hovering around, participating in, and trying to manipulate SDS. There were craft-specialized grouplets such as print-shop collectives and street theater ensembles like the one I was in. There was the secret circle of anti-draft work. There was Up Against the Wall Motherfucker, possibly a circle of hell given its offensively macho, pugnacious energy. And at the same time, in the same place as the Motherfuckers—devilish irony—there was a circle of people who were pioneers of the women's movement.

Some women, many of them active in the New Left, many of them living in New York, were then initiating and articulating what would become known as the Second Wave of feminism. (The nineteenth and early twentieth century movement focused mainly on women's suffrage was now being seen as the first wave.) Women we knew were meeting in the first consciousness-raising groups—inventing the form—where they confirmed that the obstacles to their participation, in the movement as in the world, were external and systemic, not weaknesses of their own. They were writing the modern women's movement's first essays, making its first demands to be included and heard. They may have foreseen, although I surely did not in 1967, the long seismic impact this upwelling would have. We are still experiencing the tectonic shifts now, in August of 2016, in the absurd but potent contention over gender identity and school bathrooms, for example, and in a presidential election contest between a woman and a man who freely disparages women.

Among those who talked me into joining the staff was the writer Marge Piercy, who always encouraged my writing, and whose early poems like "Unlearning to not speak," "I will not be your sickness," and "A just anger" galvanized that generation of nascent feminists. There was Michele Clark, who later became a therapist, with whom I passed hours in a corner of the regional office working on a project we called Dropout Counseling. We were trying to link up kids who were quitting school or running away from home with opportunities to do political organizing, or join a rural commune, or found a non-traditional school. People drop out of college, or out of the lives they are expected to pursue, in every era. But the Sixties were boom times; people didn't worry about finding jobs as they do now, nor did they accumulate enormous college debt. Dropping out was celebrated then, as an act of rebellion you felt you were taking in concert with thousands of others. And there was this counterculture you could drop right into.

Michele and I were trying to do social work as subversion, to people a new society with defectors from the old. We soon abandoned the effort; it was too nurturing and delicate for the combative culture maturing around us. Marge and Michele and other women in the office's orbit befriended me, fed me—real meals, even, sometimes. Their concern and support offset my general intimidation by the loudmouth guys who always sucked up most of the oxygen in the room. Maybe those women befriended me because I was younger and they saw that I lacked armor, or sensed I was closeted, or maybe just because that's what women tend to do. I thought the women's politics they were talking about made sense, and claimed to support it, although being a man I avoided contemplating it too deeply.

Women who had one foot in the New Left and one in this new feminism were torn, naturally, between two different and not especially compatible emerging visions of revolution. Already, when I first encountered them, a separatism was developing, akin to the disquieting black separatism that was also emerging, and similarly manifesting in distinct groups and strategies. As opportunities proliferated for directing their activism to feminist issues, and conducting it under their own leadership, many abandoned the male-dominated left, which included SDS. It was the same a few years later, after Stonewall in June 1969, and the founding of groups like the Gay Liberation Front and Gay Activists Alliance, when homosexuals, too, fled the left en masse (myself not included; in June 1969, I was casting my lot with the machos of Weatherman). Gay people suddenly felt free to build their own organizational platforms and raise their own issues. As women's liberation had taught, the personal was political.

Jeff could have looked back from the vantage point of 1989 and said, "So you see, it all traces right back to the Lower East Side and people we knew then like Marge and Michele, groups like New York Radical Women, and the Society for Cutting Up Men." (SCUM wasn't a real organization but a single deranged feminist, Valerie Solanas, who tried to assassinate Andy Warhol in 1968; in her wacky hyperbole and terrorist spirit, she and SCUM were a female analogue to Ben Morea and the Motherfuckers.) Except that it wouldn't have occurred to Jeff to say that. To him and the others who became leaders of Weatherman, feminism was never deeply grasped, or urgent, or much more than a nuisance.

· · ·

I missed out on the fun and billy clubs at the Columbia strike in April of '68. It had been a too-vertiginous few months since the Pentagon. I retreated to Ohio and crashed with some Antioch pals who had rented an old farmhouse, worked for a few weeks at a real farm down the road shoveling manure and digging fencepost holes in the spring sun. Still, this retreat to the country was interrupted by political reality. There was the assassination of Martin Luther King and the paroxysm of urban rebellions it set off, harrowing to observe from that pastoral distance.

Karin Ashley, another Antiochian who had been in New York, running around with Jeff, Phoebe, me, and others in the regional staff and Motherfucker circles in the preceding months, was also back on campus that spring. Karin was smart, and a bit sly. She had first arrived at school—still only seventeen, I think—boldly intent on getting immersed in radical politics, and she succeeded. I seem to recall that her first co-op job was at the SDS National Office in Chicago; no other place could have provided a deeper immersion. Now, when a meeting was called to organize a response at Antioch to what was happening at Columbia, people looked to Karin and me, thinking that because we had been SDS staff we could tell them what to do. I don't remember what we might have suggested, or if anything resulted. But I do remember that the two of us spent a few surreptitious hours on our own, talking over an idea to firebomb the office where an anthropology professor was carrying out a research project on skull shapes, funded by the Department of Defense. I had no idea what he was actually studying or what purpose his findings might have had. The whiff of eugenics and the war machine connection were incriminating enough for me. Never mind that this office was located in the basement of a timber building that housed, upstairs, the college art department, where some of our friends were students.

A day or two before we were aiming to do it, somebody else bombed the office of the draft board in the nearby town of Xenia—a clearer target, I was chagrined to note. We ditched our plan. A lot of people at Antioch assumed Karin and I had done the draft board. There were knowing winks and slaps on the back for days. It was vaguely mortifying. But secretly so. Here again, I found comfort in secrecy. Nothing actually stopped us from going ahead with our own scheme, I realize now. I also see, in this non-incident, the early stages of a developing pattern in which I call for, or can be seen to call for, confrontational acts, but somehow escape actually participating in or answering for them.

• • •

I spent the next year on the regional staff back home in Washington. On the way there, I attended SDS's annual national convention at Michigan State, where I helped fend off another incursion by Progressive Labor. This did not require me to overcome public-speaking jitters so that I could address an argument to the delegates assembled in plenary session. Not that there wasn't ideological battle going on. The Marxoid jargon spewed by PL had begun to provoke declamations of equally pretentious articles of faith from others of us. This was the meeting at which Bernardine Dohrn, who would later be a maximal leader of the Weathermen, declared herself to be a "revolutionary communist," and called for us to express solidarity—which we did, in rousing cheers and, if memory serves, an actual vote—with Enver Hoxha's Albania. I cheered, too, though at the time I knew not a thing about Albania, a dystopia that the phrase "police state" would scarcely have begun to describe. But the point of Bernardine's posturing was simply to one-up PL. My role in blocking PL's ascendance in SDS in June of '68, however, didn't involve debate, if that's what you could call it, or even posturing. It was simply a matter of stealing votes.

I don't remember who made sure that I was one of the people counting ballots alongside Karin and Phoebe, in the election of national officers who would serve for the coming year. It must have been somebody who knew how much experience we three had in furtive activities like shoplifting groceries, defacing property, and aiding draft dodgers, as well as in keeping our mouths shut. When it became clear that PL would win two of the three offices up for grabs, we managed to stuff our pockets with ballots that had been cast for their candidate for National Secretary, the organization's most publicly visible role. Once the counting was over and it was clear that the PL candidate had "lost," we race-walked across the campus and dumped the evidence in a trash bin.

An early SDS slogan had been "Let the people decide," but the days of participatory democracy were over. We were already into dirty tricks and a self-justifying culture of "by any means necessary." It was us versus them out in the world, and within SDS now, too. I felt not a scintilla of ambivalence about what we did, I am chagrined to say. And I believe now that this was the first overt act, as an indictment might term it, in a sequence of conscienceless choices and moves by those of us who would become Weatherman that ended up eviscerating SDS and leaving the organization for dead. The striking thing to me now is that Karin, Phoebe, and I were not motivated at the time by a clearly articulated political stance, or even a nonsensical one, which we had explored and agreed to, nor were we members of any disciplined cadre, although we later would all be in Weatherman.

PL did have a dogma, which was old-fashioned Marxist-Leninist boilerplate. They argued that we should move from our student base into factory jobs and from street protests to worker organizing, and that in order not to alienate the largely conservative U.S. working class, we should also get haircuts and give up drugs and other trappings of youth culture. Karin, Phoebe, and I certainly had politics in common, instinctively if not explicitly, and we obviously shared a taste for action, and for clandestinity. But our motivation then was more tribal than ideological. We fiddled that election to protect the cool kids, because we just couldn't stomach the nerds.

• • •

I spent precisely one year living back in Washington—June 30, 1968 to June 30, 1969, a symmetry of timing that seemed bizarre when everything else was so headlong and unstable. In fact, my arrival and departure dates were coincidental. Still, when I moved on next to the maelstrom of the National Office in Chicago and the founding days of Weatherman, I imbued the preciseness of that year with ineffable significance, as we did—half-seriously—with lots of things in that time of magical thinking. For example, we were inclined to hear pop music as speaking directly to us. As if the Rolling Stones were deliberately urging on our militance with lyrics from what, I noted with amusement this morning, their website calls "the album that changed everything" for the band, signifying that they had "reached their musical manhood." Ahem. Cock rock, anyone? "Everywhere I hear the sound of marching, charging feet." And, "Every cop is a criminal, and all the sinners saints." Ditto the Beatles, on *The White Album*. "Happiness is a warm gun." And, "Have you seen the bigger piggies….In their eyes there's something lacking. What they need's a damn good whacking."

We weren't the only people who were hearing voices. Charles Manson took that Beatles lyric literally and acted on it, with bloody results. Both albums were released in 1968; obviously their authors were responding to what was happening then in the world. But surely they did not have either Manson or our action faction of SDS specifically in mind. Still, half-serious also means half-credulous. Or half willfully naïve. It was willfully credulous to believe that our movement composed overwhelmingly of white college students and dropouts who ranged from moderately to extremely affluent and privileged, and were motivated perhaps above all by the personal threat that the male half of us could be drafted and sent off to that lunatic war, would transform itself into a people's army.

The thinking was even more unhinged when we imagined that Weatherman, a tiny particle of that movement—even if we could agree to fight in concert with all the other minuscule militaristic leftist spinoffs of the Sixties, and with the Black Panthers who had broad support because they not only asserted the right to armed self-defense but also provided services like free medical clinics and breakfasts for schoolkids, and even if all of us revolutionary guerrillas were supported by rampaging mobs from the ghettos and campuses—it was magical thinking to imagine that we could possibly overcome the power of the U.S. government. And magical in the extreme to think that we would then take our places as the commissars and apparatchiks of a new regime. But we weren't half-serious about these far-fetched conceits. We were dead serious, and quite delusional. It sounded as if the Stones were speaking directly to us in saying "the time is right for violent revolution."

Life in the Washington regional staff collective in that year leading up to the founding of Weatherman, however, had a homespun, industrious, almost mild quality—except at those moments of crescendo when our diligent organizing efforts successfully resulted in melees. Washington was something of a backwater on the left, without a history of industrial organizing since government had always been its industry. The likes of PL didn't invest energy there, and none of SDS' other polemicists happened to live there either, so we were somewhat isolated from the factional dynamic which was growing more bitter through the year.

The more consistent members of our fluctuating collective included Cathy Wilkerson, who had opened the regional office single-handedly the previous year. Cathy was one of those who was involved in the women's movement, but also so committed to militance and a socialist vision that she later found herself unable to elude the vortex of Weatherman. Her then boyfriend was Mike Spiegel. I'd met him the previous fall, when I was still living alone in New York—in a tiny, bleak studio Mike afterward always referred to as "that hovel." One of the SDS people I'd been getting to know called in the middle of a rainy night. He and a friend from out of town were tripping, with nowhere to go. They came and crashed at my place. Mike stuck around for another day. I thought he was only recovering from the rigors of acid, but he was also taking shelter from the press of his responsibilities. I didn't know that he had dropped out of Harvard a few months earlier to serve as SDS' National Secretary—and he didn't feel it necessary to mention, because he doesn't have that kind of ego. We've had a calm, warm friendship ever since.

Also living with us was Bill Willett, called Willie or Willett, a sex-drugs-and-rock'n'rolling hippie who had been an alienated poverty program volunteer when Cathy met and recruited him. Sober-minded John Fournelle had just dropped out of Georgetown University along with Hank Topper, who bore the mortifying capitalist cross of having a father who owned a factory. (It was a candy factory, which made this indictment hard to take too seriously.) Helen Selhorst, from a working class Baltimore family of thirteen kids, had little patience for jargon, and was skilled at high-volume meal preparation. Helen and Hank paired off midway through the year, and a few years later had a daughter they named Anna Krupskaya, after Lenin's wife. By then our Washington group had broken up and while some of us were in the Weather Underground, as their choice of a baby name suggests, they were in a more traditional Marxist-Leninist sect; Helen must have suffered some jargonesque conversations to achieve that. By then, we probably wouldn't even have spoken to each other civilly, since we spewed a different ideological nonsense. Sectarianism is that toxic. Your recent comrades become your despised enemies. But this pathetic waste of trust and connection was still in the future. In '68–69, in the D.C. regional staff, we made a home for each other and did our work, and harmony prevailed.

We rented a big, old row house. We pooled resources, but we were broke all the time. "How did we live? How did we eat?" John Fournelle asked me. Hardscrabbling suffused his feeling for the period. He recalled collecting soda bottles on the street to turn in for refunds, and one of his sharpest memories, contrastingly rich, was when a few of us stopped at my father's in Chevy Chase and ate ice cream drizzled with creme de menthe. We shoplifted groceries. We ate a lot of peanut butter and brown rice. Sometimes we found part-time jobs to supplement the erratic donations we received.

The self-imposed poverty didn't bother me. I liked the idea that I could carry everything I owned in a backpack. It enhanced that self-righteous idea of being a guerrilla, someone who could disappear nimbly without a trace. For much of my adult life I have lived close to the edge financially; I wouldn't advise becoming a writer, if you can't handle that. But I've always been confident that things would work out and I would somehow be okay. Some philosophies hold that if you believe that sort of thing about yourself fiercely enough, it will be realized. Of course, that is magical thinking, too.

In the Washington SDS house, we created a semblance of domesticity: chores done more or less responsibly, on a rotation; communal dinners around the big splintery telephone-cable spool that served as a dining table. We even partied occasionally, scraping up the price of nickel bags of pot and hits of acid and gallon jugs of Gallo Hearty Burgundy. The summer was easygoing and largely uneventful. We ran a "freedom school" for high school kids, did draft counseling. I had one chilling moment when we were gathering for an anti-draft rally in Dupont Circle. It was a hippie hangout then, and we figured we might interest a few of the idlers. A man pulled to the curb and beckoned me over; I thought he wanted to ask directions. He thrust a stack of leaflets at me through his window, then sped away. They read, "The crosshairs are on you," and were signed by the Minutemen, a right-wing paramilitary. I threw them away and never mentioned this to anybody, absurdly embarrassed that I might have been specifically targeted because of some manifest weakness. And for a while, I walked the streets feeling marked.

• • •

It was blazing hot in late August when seven or eight of us set off for a soporific two-day drive to Chicago, to join the protests at the Democratic National Convention, in our 1961 VW microbus. Cute vehicle, you might think, but it had a puny 40 horsepower, and hinged windows that only opened four inches. Chicago, however, woke us up briskly. Rather than a single demonstration, this was a series of feints and skirmishes that grew in size and violence over five days. It ended with the televised police riot outside the Conrad Hilton, the Democrats' headquarters hotel, where the chant "the whole world is watching" was born.

On our first day in town, Cathy and I left the SDS National Office (everybody called it the N.O.) to go out posting an agitprop "wall newspaper" called *The Wall/Street Journal.* We weren't aware of being followed but must have been because the minute we pasted one up, we were collared. At the station we were separated. I was put in a cell with a bearded hippie facsimile who, improbably, had a camera in his possession and tried pointing it at my face. I held my palm up in front of his lens; he was soon "released." Then I was taken to an interview room where a man in plainclothes who did not identify himself politely said that he only wanted to know our plans for the week. When I demurred he allowed, with somewhat more menace, that he was sure I wouldn't want to harm my father's State Department career. I didn't really have or know of any plans, beyond being part of the action. And if I had, I wouldn't have divulged them unless the cops had beaten them out of me. The dude with the camera, the detective's knowledge of who I was—this episode felt comic in the moment, and I was released shortly, without being charged. It felt creepier after the fact—the state's iron fist in a velvet glove.

I was busted again twice in the following days. Once it was for failing to put on the headlights as I was "racing" us to safety from a nighttime street battle in the pokey microbus. We were all escorted into the station where we contrived to sidle up to an open window, one by one, and drop through it the rocks we had put in our pockets for the purpose of throwing at police. I had a third arrest, too, I forget for what. In all these, I either wasn't charged, or the charges were dropped. Still, it was agreed that I ought to get off the street.

I spent the remaining days of the demos camped out at the N.O. helping put out more posters, making calls to raise bail money, and watching the increasingly disturbing confrontations on TV. My younger brother Higgy, who was sixteen, phoned me there. Our checked-out father had sent him to California to spend the summer with our uncle's family. Now hitchhiking home to Washington, he had been drawn to the action. In a rare gesture of family loyalty, protectively, I insisted that he come to the N.O. to get off the streets and out of the fighting, and after a few days sent him on his way home via my Antioch friends in that farmhouse where I'd spent the spring. But my family feeling only went so far. Around the same time, our mother's father died. I did not go to his funeral, and I never bothered to see my grandmother again, either.

In Chicago, once more it seemed I had avoided risks and escaped consequences. Luck? Subconscious maneuvering for self-preservation? This recurring aspect of my Sixties career made me feel vaguely inauthentic, as if I had something to hide. No more. There are things that I regret about those years. But having avoided both serious legal trouble and getting my head cracked are not among them.

• • •

After the strikes at Columbia and Paris; after the assassination of King and the ensuing eruptions of black rage; after the stunning viciousness of the cops in Chicago; after the Democrats torpedoed the peace candidacy of Senator Eugene McCarthy, who had won a plurality of primary votes, in favor of the war apologist Hubert Humphrey; after the Republicans nominated Richard Nixon who ran on a platform of "law and order," which we correctly understood to mean repression of antiwar, leftist, student, black, and

Latino activists, et cetera; after this cascade of barbarities, when the school year began in September, SDS chapter meetings were standing-room only. Students in great numbers craved to connect and react and to hear our message. And we didn't hide our politics. That wasn't necessary, because the revolutionary vision coming from SDS was utopian and vague enough for anyone to feel included in it. It could attract anybody who had a sense of indignation or a renegade urge.

In truth, there was a spectrum of visions. There were organizers whose promised future drew directly from the Marxist-Leninist tradition: an industrial economy rationalized by centralized planning; a society in which classes would disappear as everyone was equalized, in which all would participate and by which all be taken care of. If the communist mother ship, the Soviet Union, seemed too chillingly bleak a model, there was the genuinely moving example of Cuba. Cuba was easily embraced because its history and impoverishment as a U.S. quasi-colony was obvious and shameful, and also because it was nearby, colorful, musical, warm, and seductive. And in revolutionary Cuba, inspiringly, the riches of an oligarchy had been nationalized so the former peasantry could receive literacy lessons, health care, and enough to eat. At the time we didn't notice the police state aspect of the Cuban revolution.

The appeal wasn't all revolutionary economics, though. We were the New Left precisely to distinguish ourselves from fusty communist tradition. The economically unthreatened student population we were organizing among was actually more responsive to a critique about fairness and the failures of America's democratic ideals and laws. To demonstrate that, one need point no further than examples of institutional racism, which were plentiful and everywhere, or to Vietnam, where famously and repeatedly it was necessary to destroy the village in order to save it. Carl Oglesby had been SDS' national president a couple of years earlier (before the more egalitarian-sounding system of three national secretaries was adopted). (Carl had then been Antioch's "activist-scholar in residence," during my second year in college.) He had famously proclaimed to those who would call us anti-American, "Don't blame *me* for *that*. Blame those who mouthed my liberal values, and broke my American heart."

And there were gauzier dreams that some organizers, including me, wrapped all this in: visions of pastoral communalism in which the sun was always shining and the garden ever bounteous; an innocent belief in Martin Luther King's "beloved community," where decency and equality would prevail; confidence in the limitless creative power of expanded consciousness via psychedelic drugs; and all manner of stirring hallucinations embedded in the music of the moment. For me, most alluring among those was the vision in David Crosby's "Triad," first performed by Jefferson Airplane. "Sister lovers, some of you must know about water brothers, and in time, maybe others. So you see? What we can do is to try something new, that is if you're crazy too." Personally? I was hoping for water brothers.

Each of us on the D.C. staff took on some particular task, either working with one of the college chapters, or focusing on draft counseling, or in my case organizing high school kids. I was organizing at schools just like, and including, the one I had attended, but coming up the drive now in the groovy microbus, with my long hair and beads and irreverence.

To our eager audiences we on the staff—full-time, dropped-out, professional revolutionaries—must have trailed auras of enviable glamour and dedication. Surely there was an element of romance in why some people chose to follow us, romance of the puppy love variety. There was romance in the politics for sure, in both the dreamy revolutionary world we promised and the fantastic process, the fierce love-in on the barricades, we implied could bring it about. And we weren't turning people off with leaden Marxist-Leninist dogma, not in D.C., even as we increasingly studded our talk with ideas and slogans we lifted superficially and uncritically from Mao Tse-Tung, Fidel Castro, Ho Chi Minh, the Black Panthers, and other leftists and revolutionaries. But the rhetoric was not what drew people. Our attitude, increasingly wild-eyed and cocky, had some allure. But the true appeal of our organizing was the opportunity it provided people to imagine and do something with their justified anger and desperation.

That year was punctuated by several splashy actions in which we did our best to push the limits. We had a demonstration on election day in November, along with SDS across the country under the slogan, "The elections don't mean shit! Vote in the streets!" We were refused a permit, but marched anyway, disrupting traffic. During a massive national mobilization to protest Nixon's inauguration in January 1969, we were the ones throwing rocks and clods of dirt at his motorcade from the sidewalk of Pennsylvania Avenue, abandoning the more familiar political slogans as his car neared us to simply scream, "Fuck you."

In March, the mayor of San Francisco was to speak on the topic of law and order at Georgetown. The San Francisco police, on a daily basis, were savagely pummeling students at the state college there who were on strike demanding increased minority admissions and faculty hiring and an ethnic-studies program. Our Georgetown chapter led a successful disruption of the mayor's talk, which involved a brawl with conservative students who had been recruited by the school administration to stop us. The grand finale of our year's work came in May when the SDS chapters at the University of Maryland and George Washington and American Universities all seized campus buildings on the same night. Only one or two in each chapter, and we on the staff, knew the whole coordinated plan. That afternoon, the kids from Maryland ran into their counterparts from American at a hardware store, buying rope and chain for blockading doorways—the purpose of which was immediately obvious to both groups. It gave them a chance to practice the useful clandestine arts of pretending not to recognize people you know, and keeping quiet.

Yesterday, September 1, 2016, I went online to read documents from a Congressional investigation into the activities of Washington SDS during the year I was there. These include pictures of the aftermath of the takeover that May night of an office building at George Washington. Our folks trashed the place, leaving furniture smashed and overturned, files riffled and stolen. Somebody had chalked on a blackboard, "This wouldn't have happened if you listened before." It read to me more like an appeal to reason or a cry for understanding—wistful even—than a howl of defiance. But most people viewing those photos would simply see the wreckage.

Also yesterday I heard about two other things that are surely on a through-line with our actions in that spring of '69, and might never have come about if the Sixties hadn't generated so much turmoil. Georgetown University announced that it will offer preferential admission to descendents of the 272 slaves the institution owned and sold in 1838, and some other gestures of racial reconciliation. And San Francisco 49ers quarterback Colin Kaepernick seems to be starting a movement among athletes to kneel silently rather than stand with hands over hearts when the national anthem is sung before games, to call attention to police brutality and racial inequality. We were right in 1969 to spotlight racism and the inexcusable violence of the police, though we were often destructive in how we felt compelled to do it. But perhaps our strident insistence helped make possible these gestures five decades later which are so refreshingly creative and powerful.

We remained connected that year in Washington to the larger, looser community of protest and the counterculture. Still it was a time of transition out, of disengagement. We had begun to experience thrilling druglike waves of contempt for other people, rushes of our own superiority. Washington was my hometown, but I rarely sought out friends there who certainly opposed the war and racism but might not have approved of our militance. I avoided my family, too. Even within the activist world, we looked for points of disagreement rather than grounds for unity.

That counter-inaugural demonstration, like most of the mass national antiwar gatherings in those years, had been organized by the National Mobilization Committee to End the War in Vietnam. The "Mobe" was a broad coalition from many points on the political spectrum. It was certainly not advocating revolution or intending, as we were, to provoke disorder in the streets. But on the day of the inauguration, there were some fights between the SDS contingent and the police, and some arrests. I wrote a report on the event for the next issue of *New Left Notes*, the SDS national newspaper. "The reason that the pigs could perform so smoothly," I proclaimed, "was because the Mobilization marshals effectively functioned as cops." And, "It was necessary for people to threaten that they would bust up their office before they agreed to pay people's bails." Poor editing, on that last sentence. It should have read, "It was necessary for *us* to threaten that *we* would bust up their office..." Now I can see the pattern, and the preparations we were making. Each connection severed left us more defiant and alone.

2.

By June of '69 none of the schools asked to host the annual SDS convention agreed, because of the many campus disruptions we had fomented in the preceding year, and because the FBI threatened that we would do the same to them if they did. Before, national meetings took place on leafy campuses with well-lit auditoriums for plenary sessions, empty classrooms for workshops and caucuses and the occasional quickie, cafeterias and dorms for those other bodily needs of sustenance and sleep, and ample lawns and lounges for hanging out. But this time, we gathered in a seedy, echoing sports arena in a Chicago slum. There were no pleasant walks to take, if you wanted to clear your head or catch up quietly with a friend.

I guess that for sleep we crashed on the floors of church basements. What we did for food I don't recall but I can't imagine we were eating regularly. What we did ingest would have been heavy on the caffeine and sugar, which would only have contributed to the delirium that ensued. Another feature of the heightened state of conflict we now operated within was elaborate security. Arriving at the arena, people had to line up to be searched for anything that could identify them as informers, or as members of the "bourgeois press" who weren't welcome either, and for drugs and weapons. We weren't against drugs and weapons, but we didn't want to provide any excuse for a police raid. It was hot on the sidewalk in front of the hall, the air noxious with vehicle exhaust. It sometimes took hours to get inside. Nerves frayed.

Not everyone had to wait in line. I was pulled out right away by SueJan, a big, warm Texan on the National Office staff who called everybody "honey." (Her name was Susan and I remember her last name, which began with "Jan" and might have been Polish, but not how to spell it. I can't find her online to verify it and am not in touch with anybody who would know. Everybody called her SueJan.) She pressed me into working with her on the Registration and Credentials Committee. We sat at a table and interrogated people, once they had been frisked and allowed in the door, as to their membership status. Officially, we were trying to verify the identities of voting delegates, and count them. At the same time, we were making a secret tally of how many people were likely to be in the Progressive Labor camp, and how many on "our" side. As we flipped through our slowly growing stacks of registration cards, we realized with mounting distress that PL had a majority.

This kind of work, the bureaucratic part and the internally subversive part underneath it, was what lieutenants like SueJan and I often found ourselves doing at this phase in the degeneration of SDS, while our generals were elsewhere, in some closed room, engaging in the more vaunted work of drafting polemics and strategies of factional attack. I leave it to the political historians to untangle the ideological convolutions of those rants. As I have surely made clear, I have never been much concerned with doctrinal minutia, nor is it of any great importance in the telling of my story, as demonstrated by this: Though we were fond of each other and happy to conspire at the registration table, SueJan and I were loyal to a leadership of the anti-PL wing of SDS that was itself already splitting in two. By the end of this convention these cliques would come to oppose each other as bitterly as together they hated PL. SueJan and I did not end up in the same one, but the reasons for that were at least as much due to which leaders we each were better friends with as to distinctions of ideology.

It's not that there weren't real differences in the various factions' stances, although whichever one had dominated would have squandered what was valuable about SDS to some degree, by being so unyieldingly opinionated if for no other reason. I do not argue that there's no use in having what doctrinaire leftists call an analysis, meaning a grand theory of how the world works. I don't say that there's no value in advancing strategic ideas for improving the world. But the fallacy of ideological leftism, or of any ideological ism, is to believe that an interpretation of the world's condition and a strategy for addressing it could possibly be perfect, all-encompassing, capable of being articulated at one moment and remaining apt over time.

The world is too complex and irrational to be intellectualized and reduced like that. Believing that it can be is at once an expression of arrogance and a mask for the fear of weakness—a refusal to acknowledge the truth that our abilities to understand and act are limited, pitifully so. But we were young in 1969. It is in the nature of youth to be idealistic—but also at times arrogant; those traits can get things done, but they can also mislead. SDS was a locus of power and reach, what we would call today a platform. We all desperately wanted to affect world events, so SDS seemed a prize worth fighting each other for. But the high ideals of the New Left were succumbing to the glorious leftist tradition of paranoid and malicious sectarianism. The Bolsheviks versus the Mensheviks versus the Trotskyists. The various mind-numbing but lethal campaigns within communist parties against "revisionists" and "deviationists." I believe that although we were of the New Left, those of us at the center of SDS by this time had come to believe that adopting and perpetuating this mode of behavior would validate us, prove our superior purity and bona fides.

After the convention, I did spend another day or two with SueJan, because I immediately moved to Chicago to work at the National Office, and she was obliged—through gritted teeth, no more "honey"—to show me the ropes. Then I never saw her again, and as long as I remained an arrogant revolutionary I wouldn't have given her the time of day if I had.

• • •

At the convention, after a couple of days of shouting each other hoarse, the anti-PL side, aware that we did not have the voting strength to hold on to the organization, redefined the situation by walking out. Oddly, the arena had two halls, as if it had been chosen with this eventuality in mind—we only had to step through a doorway to reconvene without our nemesis—but surely that was coincidental. There we voted to "kick out" Progressive Labor. But the non-PL national leadership contained two mutually hostile factions. At the convention, one put forth a position paper titled with a line from Bob Dylan: "You don't need a weatherman to know which way the wind blows." This was the bad seed that effloresced into Weatherman. The other's screed was entitled "Revolutionary Youth Movement II," following on an earlier document six months earlier that argued that young people would be the agents of revolution; they got called RYM II for short.

This conflict had been brewing over the preceding months, in an atmosphere of growing mistrust and secrecy. Few people were aware of it before the convention. Mike Spiegel has told me that he and Cathy Wilkerson, the only people from our Washington scene considered by the national heavyweights to be politically consequential, were romanced by each group. I knew something was going on, but only because of my social connections and nose for intrigue. I knew that Jeff, a member of the cabal that became Weatherman, kept going to Chicago for meetings he wouldn't talk about. And Willett, who had left D.C. in the spring to help out at the N.O., and whose friendships and cheekiness naturally pulled him in the same direction though he wasn't part of the in-group, had gleefully dubbed the two blocs the BPC, or Beautiful People's Commune, and the RDC, or Running Dogs Collective. ("Running dogs" was a commonplace slander among Maoists—including the frenzied mobs of the Great Proletarian Cultural Revolution who were at that very moment terrorizing the already browbeaten masses of China. It meant lackeys and pariahs, as in, "running dogs of imperialism.") In the months to come, we Weatherpeople routinely called our former friends and comrades of RYM II "running dogs." Or just "the dogs," which felt even more dismissive and fun to say. At the convention, following the walkout, the alliance of the two groups to oust PL instantly fell apart. Like, the very same day. Three signers of the Weatherman paper were elected to be national officers for the coming year. One of them was my friend and patron Jeff.

Weatherman looked to what we called America's Third World internal colonies, and to militants arising from them, like the Black Panther Party, to lead. We saw our role as enlisting radicalized young whites—the dropouts, street kids, countercultural dreamers, military deserters—in an army of support. And thanks to the increasingly frenzied rhetoric of rebellion and the invasive cancer of Marxist ideology, it no longer seemed legitimate to us to organize a primarily student-based movement. So those of us who had been in Washington ceased to value the movement we had built there, and our household was breaking up.

Cathy and Mike were getting ready to travel across the South, looking for somewhere to settle and organize. John, Hank, and Helen, along with several people from our college chapters, were moving together to gritty industrial Baltimore, to get factory jobs and organize workers. I didn't have a plan. Jeff implored me to come to the National Office. "I need you," he said. "I need somebody there I can trust when I'm traveling." Willett was already in Chicago. Jeff and Phoebe would be there now, too. We could all share an apartment. I imagined a new household, even more familial than the collective house in D.C. "I want to come home and you've cooked dinner," Jeff said. That was seductive. Plus, I would have an important job, with a title—Assistant National Secretary—and proximity to power and, as we saw it, the vortex of history. If I didn't agree to Jeff's request, I would have to put effort into a strategy for my own life, a solitary and more frightening challenge. But I believed our own fantastic vision. By now, at twenty-one, I saw my life unfolding in the revolution, and fully expected that the revolution would give me a life. Like, for the rest of my life.

So I found us a roomy, agreeably funky apartment, on the top floor of a building with a turret at its corner. From the place SueJan was vacating to return to Texas, we acquired a round oak dining table that we put in the circular alcove the turret made in our living room. We had a few languid suppers there, windows open to the hazy sunset. There were other people we knew in the neighborhood; we walked to somebody's place to drink beer and watch the first moon landing. I went off every morning to the office, like a regular person. For a minute or two, I really expected to have a sort of normal life. How did this ever reconcile with our dreams of havoc and pitched battle?

• • •

The office was in a spacious three-story building that had obviously been built in anticipation of more presentable environs than the corner of Madison and Ashland, which by 1969 was the frontier between seedy Skid Row and the impoverished black West Side. The smaller and scruffier local office of the Black Panther Party was just a few blocks down Madison Street in that direction. Downstairs of us there were storefronts, including a tavern and liquor store, and a cheap Mexican restaurant, both much frequented by SDS staff. Double doors from the sidewalk opened onto a wide stairway, at the head of which a broad, windowed hall led to high-ceilinged offices, and a second staircase to the top floor. I had a room of my own that overlooked the street and the property across the way, which had been cleared for an unbuilt urban renewal project and was now a meadow of rubble and rangy weeds. There were tall casement windows that opened inward. I remember filmy white curtains drifting in and out, but surely I have invented this mellowing detail. In my desk drawer, one of my former comrades reminded me years later, I usually kept a pint of cheap Scotch, purchased downstairs.

We were not at first the building's only occupants. The Chicago Peace Council, an antiwar alliance, had offices there for a while. And a naturopath, Dr. Otha Briscoe, had his clinic on the top floor. But our presence already dominated. For at least a year already, the SDS office had never been left unoccupied; staffers drew night duty by rotation. And the first of many fortifications had already been applied to the glass front doors. They were routinely kept locked. People wishing to enter would ring, and someone would come to the top of the stairs to see who was there before buzzing them in. We were afraid the cops would want to get in, to take our files and smash our typesetting machines and expensive offset printing press. There had already been one raid, under the pretext that a fire had been reported, when five of the previous year's staff were arrested on charges that were later dropped; after that event, steel brackets had been fixed to the doorjambs, and a two-by-four laid across the doors to prevent their being battered in.

We were also under more or less constant siege by a gang of little kids. Slippery as eels, they would hide just out of sight while one of Dr. Otha Briscoe's elderly patients was waiting to be buzzed in, then race up the stairs. They were around seven or eight years old, cute and spunky. They had no idea what we were about. "S damn D," they called us, and "S dewey." They began to climb the fire escapes and wriggle in through back windows; they seemed able to drop in from the roof. They would whip through and lift whatever they could—purses, small pieces of office equipment. It was exasperating, and surreal. They began to seem less cute and more menacing. Were they just bored, unsupervised children who found us weird and entertaining, and easy targets? Were the cops encouraging them?

We responded with added defenses. We boarded up the windows to the fire escapes. We put a complicated series of locks on all the interior doors. After a while we installed a heavy metal cage with a locking gate on the landing halfway up the stairs, so that people could be buzzed in from above but only get further into the building when someone went down to open the gate. Later still we had the front doors clad in sheet metal, leaving only a small peephole. Now two people were required to answer the door. One went all the way to the bottom to check through the peephole and then open the outside door, while the second waited to re-open the gate halfway up.

Possibly I have scrambled the order in which this accretion of armor went into place, but I remember with grim clarity the evolving state-of-war mentality it represented, and the attenuation of contact with the world. Each new layer of defense was a response to some escalation, either by the kids or the police. The cops returned several times and were never in fact prevented by any of this hardware from coming in when they wanted to. There's something that's persuasive about a loaded service revolver. With each window nailed shut, each pane smashed and boarded over, our light and air and view of the world contracted.

Through it all, Dr. Otha Briscoe's ailing clients, though dwindling in number for perhaps understandable reasons, presented themselves at the entry and made their halting progress through our breastworks and up the two flights to receive their herbal infusions and high colonics.

• • •

Early yesterday, a fast, wild storm propelled the sluggish late summer heat away from here, where Peter and I live, in the Hudson Valley. Just like that, rinsed and refreshed, it became the precious first dazzling-blue early-autumn day. I was reading on the deck when a small single-engine plane passed overhead, its motor reminiscent of a lawnmower, or of that trick we used to do as kids with our bikes, fixing a playing card to a strut with a wooden clothespin so that it slapped every spoke of the turning rear wheel to make a whirr we pretended was the sound of a motorcycle.

Maybe this is no longer true, or maybe I simply no longer notice, but it occurred to me that when I was growing up in Chevy Chase, light planes with engines sounding like lawnmowers, or like toys, crossed the sky far more often—a frequent recurring delight, mainly perhaps for little boys who are hard-wired to love any machine with wheels or wings. Or maybe I remember those planes' wonderfully ordinary ever-presence because our children's books were filled with imagery of then-modern vehicles in motion. Was there a publishing house that slapped the same illustration into all its books?

Half of mine, in memory at least, had endpapers depicting the city as what we might now call a multi-modal transportation hub. Small single-engine planes, and curvaceous prop-driven airliners with triple tails, and silvery blimps all soar above the skyscrapers; steadfast and workaday subway trains chug across bridges; an overpass bearing a mannerly traffic of bulbous autos and trucks arcs over the railyard, where a gleaming transcontinental stream-liner with glassed observation domes must be just about to call all aboard; and ferries, tugs, stately three-stacked liners with graceful prows, and stirring, reassuring fire and police boats are all busy in the harbor. Did I mention the sunbeams and pillowy clouds?

This was a world-of-wonders version of New York City, of course, rendered safe for consumption by minors. In New York you can still get similar vistas, at least as multi-modal and kinetic if less idealized and benign, from any bridge or waterfront site that makes a wide view possible, or from a high floor in a tower. The date yesterday, when I was lulled into this reverie by the sound of that light airplane, that precious first dazzling-blue early-autumn day where we live two hours north of New York, happened to be September 11, 2016. Yes, it was that same flawless, promising September 11 weather. Rest in peace.

I didn't tell you about another guerrilla theater piece I was part of. Some of those same arty pranksters who did the fake self-immolation in front of the Antioch cafeteria found ourselves together in New York toward the end of 1967. This was right after I'd joined the SDS staff, nearly two years before the emergence of Weatherman. We were planning to crash a remote-controlled toy plane into the televised dropping ball in Times Square at fifteen seconds before midnight on New Year's Eve, and then release a statement condemning the U.S. presence in Vietnam. This is another story of brilliant agitprop conception, excellent clandestine practice, and glib indifference to possible consequences. If it hadn't been below freezing, when those tiny engines don't like to start—one of many details we didn't trouble to think through—we might have brought it off and altered the course of history, in ways I don't like to imagine. But I don't have to imagine them. We are now quite familiar with clandestine actions, even actions meant to be only symbolic, that can have lasting consequences for the innocents directly affected and ultimately for everyone else. Real aircraft crashing into tall buildings are only the most spectacular example. So far.

Sometimes the consequences do not seem immediately so grave because they aren't in themselves sensational, instead having long, slow but still awful impacts on how we live. I have described some of the security measures we took in SDS—had to take—to protect ourselves from the police and their hench-persons, possibly including hench-children, as our political situation became ever more bellicose. Given that yesterday was September 11, I have been thinking about all that has been put in place by governments, corporations, and other institutions to protect against terrorism: those rules, procedures, thought processes, and technologies demanded by the forever war—including, to my bleak amusement, the new favorite toy aircraft of little boys, the drone. But today especially I am remembering what the world was like before all of this superstructure of fear was forced into being.

Perhaps you can't recall the lost world where, for example, airports were so wide open and welcoming that teenagers like me visited them on dates, just for the free entertainment that included planes taking off and landing, unusually dressed people speaking foreign tongues, and the fantasy of exotic travel. I, of course, an art snob, took my high school dates only to Dulles Airport because it was the latest masterwork of architect Eero Saarinen—although I always loved airports and planes, or did when they were open and welcoming, and when air travel was still exotic and not so fraught. When I lived in Taipei my future stepbrother David Birnbaum and I used to ride our bikes to the airport and right out onto the tarmac, to play in the cockpits of unlocked and unwatched DC-4 and DC-6 airliners that would later in the day perhaps lumber off loaded with trusting passengers for Tokyo or Hong Kong.

The beginning of the end for that openness was the invention of the guerrilla weapon of airliner hijackings, in July 1968. Militants from the Popular Front for the Liberation of Palestine forced an El Al flight to land in Algiers, where after forty days of negotiations both they and their Israeli hostages went free. Wow! A new tactic! And so easy to do! The Israelis never again negotiated with hijackers; El Al famously has the most rigorous security of any airline in the world. But in the following few years there were many more hijackings. I was going to count them up from a list on Wikipedia and got dizzy scrolling at about thirty-five, but you get the idea. Some of these were perpetrated by disturbed persons, some by apolitical crafty ones simply seeking to ransom the planes and their human cargos, and quite a few by insurgents of various stripes, including many revolutionaries from the Americas who sought passage to asylum in Cuba.

My vertigo has cleared, so I can note that by 1973 the hijacking rate dropped precipitously because, presumably, by then metal detectors and other efforts at control had been installed at the world's airports. But it was still quite awhile before body searches, or shoe removal, or the inspection of passengers' three-ounce toiletry collections were instigated. Things tightened up incrementally over many years, so much so that even those who were adults in the vanished pre-security world might not remember that you didn't even need ID to board a plane, or to buy a ticket. It was not unusual to buy one when you were already at the airport with your bags rather than in advance, which you must do now unless you want to attract scrutiny. You could pay for air tickets in cash, too, without raising the slightest suspicion. It just wasn't a suspicious time. If you were asked for ID at the airport back then, it was probably because you were paying by check, not for surveillance purposes. Your ID wouldn't have been of much immediate value to security officialdom anyway, because nothing was digitized and the internet didn't exist. This was useful if you were pretending to be someone else, let's say to avoid facing charges, or because you were part of a secret organization conspiring to plant bombs, and you needed to fly someplace.

The earliest versions of credit cards existed by 1969 but it was more typical not to have one, and debit cards were a thing of the future. No bank cards meant no digital money trail, and no internet or cell phones meant no digital communications record, although it made staying in touch rather harder. If you needed to discuss illegal doings with people in hiding, you might have to pre-arrange times for calls weeks ahead, and make the calls between two pay phones. Landlines, including pay phones, could be tapped, of course, but not if the tappers didn't know which ones to listen in on. Also, voice recognition software didn't exist, and neither did CCTV cameras. For written communication, if you were a person of no fixed address, or no address you wanted anyone to know, you could have things sent to you at General Delivery in some town where the postmistress was no more suspicious than the airline clerks, if you behaved unsuspiciously. Or you could rely on the instant and ever-available camaraderie of the counterculture to find somebody who would believe a concocted reason why you needed to get mail at their place. That person might also be perfectly willing to let you leave a suitcase, or whatever, until you passed back through to collect your letter. And for your shorter term storage needs, every airport, train station, intercity bus terminal, and many other locations had coin-operated lockers.

Of course, it's unwise to go around without identification. You might be stopped for neglecting to signal a left turn. But fake ID wasn't difficult to obtain. There was always the dead-baby-birth-certificate method, for descriptions of which you can read any number of thrillers or refer to the William Crandall storyline in *The Americans*. There were also bumbling cops, who might have been good enough at catching robbers and cracking heads but lacked counterinsurgency skills. Suppose you were picking up a letter at General Delivery in Mayberry, and someone suggested to Deputy Barney Fife that you vaguely resembled the blurred photo on a wanted poster pinned to the post office bulletin board. "Hey, Barney, doesn't she look a little like that Bernardine Dohrn?" "'Scuse me, may I see your driver's license? Thank you kindly, ma'am." "Nah, wasn't her. License says her name is Sadie Hawkins."

I wonder whether we could have built a clandestine organization and successfully maintained it for as long as we did, while the authorities never stopped trying to find us, if we had been living under the surveillance and security conditions in place today. Of course, unlike us, the terrorists of today generally don't mind getting caught or killed. Some of them have been promised one-way tickets to a First Class paradise, and all of them seem mainly focused on the splashy event itself, not what comes after. A heavenly afterlife and/or pixelated immortality online are apparently future enough for them.

• • •

Through the summer and into the fall of 1969, we forged ourselves into an infantry of swaggering kamikazes dedicated to the ideas in the Weatherman position paper. Every effort was aimed toward a series of demonstrations we called for Chicago in October. They became known after the fact as the Days of Rage, although in building for it we just called them "the National Action." Our goal was to get tens of thousands of angry young people fighting the cops in the streets. In the event, only about four hundred people actually participated, maybe fewer. There was an opening night salvo when our troops ran through a fancy neighborhood trashing things and attacking the cops, who responded with shotguns, wounding eleven, and arrested more than sixty. A couple of actions planned for the following days didn't go forward at all—one was defused by the police as people were gathering, and we canceled another out of fear because the National Guard had been called out. The final day's march was another melee, with numerous injuries and mass arrests. Altogether, considering our inflated vision of it, the Days of Rage was a spectacular failure. So, smarting from our abandonment by the movement we had alienated and from the failure of our fantasized masses of followers to materialize, we in turn abandoned the movement and the masses in a huff. Obviously, nobody else was as committed as we were! That's when we began preparing to go underground.

This spoiled-brat, feelings-hurt motivation for such a consequential step was obscured behind our overblown rhetoric about the need for armed action. We pointed for justification—and reflected glory—to revolutions, such as the Cubans', that started with small, clandestine military ventures. We also rationalized the intention to go underground as a refusal to surrender. Many of our members accrued felony charges for things like mob action and assaulting an officer, and didn't want to face trials and jail. But our unwillingness to admit that our strategy had been a farce—that is, our shame at having talked so big and delivered so little—would also be a powerful impetus.

Over that summer leading up to the Days of Rage, we built a network of collectives in half a dozen cities; membership was somewhat fluid during those months, as some people bailed out and others were recruited, but I don't believe there were ever more than 200 or maybe 250 members. They were disciplined to a leadership group that we cutely called the Weather Bureau. At first, this consisted of the authors of the Weatherman position paper, though its membership evolved. The fact that three of them—Jeff, Mark Rudd, and Bill Ayers—had been elected at the convention to be the national officers of SDS, quickly took on a different meaning. Now it was as if this was just their assignment by the junta to which they belonged. The three officers were not responding to, or acting as if responsible to, the membership organization they nominally headed. Rather, the Weather Bureau was using SDS as a resource for implementing its own strategy. Other members of the Weather Bureau made themselves just as free to stride into the office, use the facilities, and tell us on the staff what to do. Not all of them did so; not all had a drive for personal power, and that was one reason some were cut from the Bureau. Not insignificantly, while there had been two women among the eleven signers of the position paper, Karin Ashley and Bernardine Dohrn, Karin was very quickly kicked off the Weather Bureau and Bernardine remained the only female member. (In the fall another woman was brought on, for cosmetic reasons I should think. She also didn't last long, most likely because she was a nascent lesbian feminist.)

The local groups that became Weather collectives had originally been meant as short-term organizing projects. Many who joined them were students expecting to return to college in the fall. But by fall our sense of reality was so skewed that for many, the idea of resuming life as a student would have been as inconceivable as volunteering to become a police informer. This first incarnation of Weatherman, as a public and visible organization, was nicknamed by someone—me, I think—the Weather Machine. This image gave us something to keep in mind as we subordinated our individual wills and learned to function like cogs and gears.

We didn't consider its other implication, the repetitive, controlled, mechanistic way we were thinking.

At the N.O., where I was, there was a staff that fluctuated in number between perhaps half a dozen and a dozen people. From there, the transformation of the summer projects into the Machine only reached us in anecdotes and rumors of bizarre and thrilling and scary goings-on. We began to hear of marathon meetings, "criticism/self-criticism" sessions that lasted until dawn. This was a technique appropriated from the Cultural Revolution then going on in China, aimed at beating the bourgeois individualism and wimpiness out of each other. For example, out on the street you were supposed to "lay down" the correct "raps," as if upon hearing the perfect formulation, strangers would magically abandon their own lives and join up. If your rhetoric hadn't been perfectly congruent with what the leadership was promulgating at the moment, that could be the focus of a criticism. Whatever you'd said would be picked apart—along with your self-esteem—and you were expected to recant, repent, and parrot back the right phraseology. Worse, perhaps, would be to have appeared weak. "A lot of those criticism sessions grew out of how you performed that morning leafleting, or in some confrontation with the cops. Everyone doubted themselves. I was really scared on the street," Mike remembered. Of course, it would have been rational to fear physical combat with the police. But thinking rationally wasn't possible, once you'd committed to meekly following orders and forcing yourself to be something you were not.

We heard that collective members were learning karate. There were also tales of erupting promiscuity. And we would sometimes receive surprising news that a person who had been a trusted cadre had been "offed"—ghetto slang for "killed"—and was now a non-person with whom nobody should interact. Occasionally, following one of those torturous criticism sessions, the non-person was liable just as surprisingly to be rehabilitated. Take, for example, my friend Phoebe. She had agreed to move to Chicago with Jeff, but not to be a National Office drudge. So she began to work with the Chicago summer project. Soon after that, she moved out of our apartment and into the collective's digs, and suddenly I never saw her. Then came the disturbing word that she had split for California. It was implied that she had freaked out, been too weak or unwilling to handle the internal dynamic. She had also resisted the campaign that was instigated by the virtually all-male leadership to "smash monogamy"—resisted, that is, having her relationship with Jeff broken up.

Smashing monogamy was justified as a way to free girlfriends from the domination of their boyfriends, but it also had the effect of freeing previously attached women to be sexually available to the leaders, or any other guy who felt empowered to coerce them. A week or so after disappearing, Phoebe phoned the N.O. Whoever answered the call recognized the delicacy of this matter—non-person she may now have been, but she was still possibly Jeff's non-person. He was elsewhere, so the call was given to me. She said she was in San Francisco, but coming back. She was just calling so that somebody would meet her flight. She said she was fine, but she didn't sound fine. She sounded flat, and hung up fast. Later that day I happened to see a Weather Bureau member. "Will you let her back in?" I asked him. "Oh, sure," he replied, "but first we smash." Maybe he only meant "smash her relationship with Jeff," but it felt more like "smash her" entirely, destroy her sense of herself as an independent person.

Cathy and Mike had left Washington after the June convention, and were driving through the South, visiting organizers and underground newspaper staffs. A few weeks into their trip they phoned the N.O. to see what was doing. "We were told, 'You two had better get up here, there's really important work going on,'" Mike recalled, years later. "They wanted us to join the Chicago collective. But our loyalty to Weatherman was in doubt." Cathy, when I spoke with her in 1989, described their initiation bitterly. She had penned the only criticism of the Weatherman position paper that ever found its way into the pages of *New Left Notes*; she managed that only because she wrote it immediately after the convention, before all internal debate had been squelched. She had the nerve to lead with, "The inability of the Weatherman proposal to include an organic analysis of male supremacy..." for which she paid, when she got to Chicago. She was put through "a 48-hour marathon criticism session," she told me. "I had to recant my whole critique. When it was over, I was a dishrag."

Cathy is not a dishrag. Neither is Naomi Jaffe, whom I first knew back in New York SDS. At a Weatherman conference that summer, she was convinced to join. She walked away from a teaching job and her apartment—the same apartment Jeff, Phoebe, and I had shared on the Lower East Side, as it happens—literally never going back. I looked her up in '89, and she told me, "I was freaked out by what I had been hearing from Chicago. 'Either you accept our analysis and accept this level of rage, or we will write you out of the revolution.' And we were going to have to follow not just this line, but these people." Why would individuals of strong character like Naomi, Mike, Cathy, Phoebe, and me submit to such humiliations, suspend our powers of critical thinking, and let ourselves be bossed around? What made us so willing to trash people no worse than ourselves, and take orders from people no smarter? The organization we created was a vehicle for our politics. But its peculiar nature was enabled not so much by the ideology as by the psychic crisis created within each of us by that ideology.

Weatherman held that in making a revolution, not only would black people be the vanguard but that "the blacks could do it alone." This was more than a challenge to the arrogance of white leftists, it was a profound invalidation: We were not only not primary, we were not even necessary. The acknowledgment of white privilege, an enormously important understanding that was new to most of us at the time, also permeated Weather thinking. But it became a club with which to beat ourselves up: we were coddled, and whiteness would always give us an easy out; we were racists objectively and inevitably simply by dint of being white in a racist society. There's truth to that, and value in realizing it. It makes possible an understanding of the nuances, and insidiousness, of racism both within us as individuals and in the structure of society. We, though, did not examine nuances. We leapt from this insight to judging ourselves to be worthless, along with every other white person in the country. Hence the despair and bitterness with which we took such crazy risks with our lives, and with the lives of others. But here was a group of people who were so confident—or unreflective, or power hungry—that they could promulgate these ideas without themselves being similarly debilitated. Following their leadership would be our path to rehabilitation.

No one involved, however—except the undercover cops—set out on a path of political activism with any less idealism and heart than I had at thirteen when I joined that picket line. And at the core of the original Weatherman position paper were humane and passionate convictions. Its authors understood that the war in Vietnam—and unnecessary American military meddling in other countries, in general—was a tragic blunder. And they knew that for this country racism is central to the history, and the biggest challenge. Both observations remain demonstrably true today. The leaders I criticize were right to insist on these ideas. Their failure was not in their motivations to activism, or in their instinctive radicalism and boldness, or or in their analysis—well, not in those two elements of their analysis. But they lacked humility. They liked being right way too much. They were not saints, as most leaders of most movements, even righteous ones, turn out not to be. They aren't saints, and this isn't heaven.

So in the Weather Machine we created a structure that perpetuated, endlessly and with no possible resolution, repeated mood swings between cockiness and self-loathing. We could strut around like bullies all day, and cower and pule before our hierophants in the evening. The breaking down of self-esteem, the abdication of critical judgment, the omnipotent leadership, the not-quite-free free love, the ever-present threat of banishment: We didn't identify our organization as a cult, but I guess people in cults generally don't.

• • •

Working in the National Office, my situation differed considerably from that of the collective members. I had my own bedroom in our decent-enough apartment, my own pleasant-enough office at the N.O. with a door I could close, while privacy was becoming a memory for those in the collectives. I had cars to use. I had access to money, since I did the banking; I thought nothing of skimming off a few bucks when I was out running errands to buy myself a meal, while collective members were subsisting on peanut butter. Certainly I answered to the leadership, and carried out their plans, but they were mostly not present. And I had a staff of my own to boss around.

Oddly, in the context of forced collectivization, I moved through my days largely alone. We didn't have criticism marathons at the N.O. until later. I was protected from much of the weirder internal culture that was developing. And I was not expected to venture forth every day, as the collective members were, on "organizing" forays that could get me into trouble; actually, it was explicit that I should not get in trouble, so that I could continue to keep the office running, the membership dues coming in—and being appropriated—the publications printed and distributed, the bail money raised for when others got busted. Once again, I was somehow escaping the big risks and consequences. As usual, I felt less than authentic because of this, though I also felt relieved.

Within a very short time I also became the editor of *New Left Notes* and effectively, as the role is named today in that industry, creative director of our entire publishing operation. People sometimes actually referred to me as the Minister of Propaganda. I had no training in journalism, but we weren't doing journalism, and I did have my instincts for agitprop. Compared to the exuberant and often gorgeous layouts of the underground papers of the era, *New Left Notes* had previously been sober and type-heavy, but the graphics guerrillas were in charge now.

On the cover of an issue we put out in midsummer, our National Action slogan "Bring the War Home" was printed above a suggestion for how to do just that: a photo and caption picked up from another underground paper, but that apparently first appeared in *Life* magazine in 1947. It was the caption we really liked. "With a defiant smile, 5-year-old Marion Delgado shows how he placed a 25-pound concrete slab on the tracks and wrecked a passenger train." Little Marion has a smart aleck's crooked grin, and the face of a manipulator. He was welcomed in Weatherland with war whoops and cheers, and immediately became everybody's alter ego. If you needed to find somebody at the airport, you would have Marion Delgado paged. In later issues, we listed Marion Delgado as the editor.

There is an archive of SDS ephemera at the University of Wisconsin, consisting mostly of detritus rescued from the N.O. when Weatherman abandoned the building, in early 1970, in the rush underground. I spent a few days picking through those files, in 1989. There I found notes to me from people out in the collectives, sending samples of their leaflets or ordering literature from us, all signed Marion Delgado. Marion Delgado later turned up as a possible alias on wanted posters for Weather fugitives. I've always retained a sharp memory of the image of the kid in his adorable overalls and striped t-shirt, balancing the hunk of cement on the track. But I had misremembered the caption as saying that he derailed a "troop train" or a "munitions train." Nope. It was a passenger train.

That same issue of the paper contained a lengthy report from our collective in Detroit, "Break on through to the Other Side"—another title ripped off from a rock-and-roll lyric. It recounts a series of emblematic Weather-collective actions of the period. On a Saturday afternoon, the group descended on a beach crowded with white working class kids, swept through handing out National Action leaflets, and then planted in the sand the flag of the Vietnamese National Liberation Front, the Communist enemy of the U.S. A crowd gathered and a fight broke out, perhaps starting with some riled-up Nam vets. "Sticking together as a group, we fought the attackers to a standstill and left the beach chanting," the writer reported, going on to evaluate the event: "We created a tremendous impact on the beach because we confronted kids with the fact that it's a political world...[Later] one of our people talked to a motorcycle dude who fought against us at the beach while they were both waiting in line to apply for a job at Chrysler. He had read the leaflet since the fight and dug on going to Chicago and bringing his friends."

Another action was held up as an exemplary show of women's liberation. Nine women from the collective invaded a classroom at a community college while students were taking a final exam. They barricaded the door, chanted slogans, handed out National Action leaflets and lectured their captives. "Some men got uptight and tried to charge the door in order to get out and call the pigs. These pig agents were dealt with while a...woman continued to rap to the people in their seats about Chicago and the necessity to take sides with the peoples of the world." (A different account by a participant was more explicit: the Weatherwomen "responded to such an exhibition of male chauvinism and general pig behavior by attacking the men with karate.") The Detroit collective's report described their leafleting efforts at rock concerts, drive-in burger joints, and schools. "Many of the kids we have rapped with are coming along with us on our actions, and some have become full-blown organizers for the National Action," it declares. It must have been the article's glib closing sentence that gave rise to a happy rumor among Weatherpeople that our Detroit group would be chartering a train to bring people to the demonstration in October. "The thousands of Motor City kids who come with us to Chicago will know just what business needs to be done..." As if by magic.

In our hands, *New Left Notes* metastasized. It was no longer a platform for news and debate, but solely a publicity tool for our National Action, no longer reliably published every two weeks, now just whenever we got it together. Some issues were conceived for "mass distribution" and shipped in bundles via Greyhound freight, by the thousands, to Weatherpeople around the country for handing out at the beaches and burger joints where the revolutionary youth were supposedly awaiting delivery. On the cover of the first one of these was a grainy enlarged photo from the People's Park clashes in Berkeley the previous spring. Five or six guys are turning over a cop car, the knobby end of a wooden police barrier protruding through its smashed windshield like a broken bone through flesh. Screened over the image in blocky red type—the first time the SDS paper had ever used color—was our slogan "Bring the War Home."

By this we meant both that the war in Vietnam should end and that a revolutionary civil war in the U.S. should begin. For the name of this publication we lifted James Baldwin's title, *The Fire Next Time*, enraptured by the idea of things burning. The only Baldwin I had read then—and had felt compelled to do so furtively—was his novel of gay exile, *Giovanni's Room*. Back when fear of myself as gay was a constant source of turmoil and shame, a glimpse like that of self-accepting homosexuality, even of that doomed relationship in a distant place, was a kind of promise. Years later, when I did read *The Fire Next Time*, I couldn't help returning to this: "People always seem to band together in accordance to a principle that has nothing to do with love, a principle that releases them from personal responsibility."

Our own offset presses could turn out leaflets, posters, and brochures, but not multi-page publications on newsprint in runs of thousands. Maybe it was that provocative first issue of *The Fire Next Time*, or maybe pressure from the likes of the FBI, or both, that caused our printer to refuse any more of our jobs. We found another, a family-owned shop with the dedication to free speech that is a tradition in the printing trade. By the time we finally ran SDS into the ground a few months later, they were among the few outsiders we still had any connection with. Inconveniently, they were a three-hour drive north, in Wisconsin. Now every time we put out an issue, somebody had to make this trip, either hanging around up there for the two days it took them to do the job, or else returning to Chicago and almost immediately going back again. It was expensive and aggravating and a waste of time, though it was nice to get out of the city to someplace green. The printer and his wife seemed to see only our best side, and willfully ignored the rest. I remember them taking us into their kitchen for cookies and milk. But the cookies and milk are probably a trick of memory.

• • •

Those of us in the N.O. felt less than valid because we weren't out picking fights, but we still had plenty in common with our comrades in the city collectives. All of us in the Weather Machine were trying to reinvent ourselves as self-sacrificing guerrillas. This was enhanced by our material circumstances. So acutely aware of suffering and starvation elsewhere, we created for ourselves a parallel environment of deprivation, which only made it harder to think clearly.

The typical Weather collective house was virtually bare, just an old couch or some kitchen chairs rescued from the trash for living room furniture, for use during those endless meetings when most people had to sit on the floor. An inadequate number of mattresses would carpet an attic or bedroom floor, on which everybody slept, piling up. Mike recalls stashing his dwindling personal effects in an open suitcase shoved in a corner. "You had your clean dirties and your dirty dirties, and your dirty-clean dirties, and you sorted through the piles every day and tried to find something you could put on. Who could make time to go to the laundromat?" Naomi told me, "We were so absorbed in what we were doing that eating was insignificant. I remember stealing groceries, because that was a 'political act,' but I don't remember eating them."

Stella Blank worked in the N.O. with me. (That's not her real name, which shows up almost nowhere if you search it plus the word "weather." She spoke with me in 1989, but asked that I not identify her. There are a few other people to whom I will give aliases because they, too, do not show up in the first pages of an online search, I haven't seen them in forty-five years, and have no idea of their situations. They weren't leaders, they're not famous as ex-revolutionaries, and it's not up to me to out them.) Stella remembered subsisting for days at a time on Cream of Wheat cooked over a hotplate in the office. "Once you gave the rest of us on the N.O. staff $20 or $30," she reminded me. "We took the Madison Street bus downtown to one of those horrible steak-houses where you stood in line for a greasy slab of meat and baked potato and wilted salad, for $2.99. We had exactly enough money to have a meal. It felt amazing to actually have food like that, and to get out of that office."

For the N.O. staff we maintained several apartments, but had to take turns staying awake all night at the office, on watch. Ultimately we lost the apartments. Mine had to be abandoned after the Saturday night when we had a loud party attended by N.O. staff and members of the Chicago collective, a sort of compensatory explosion of bawdiness after the everyday self-denial. At that table in the round alcove where all the windows were open, two members of the Weather Bureau got into a loud, obscenity-laced argument. Their screaming provoked some of the middle-aged greasers who hung out at the tavern on the building's ground floor to come upstairs to pick a fight with us. Some Weatherperson greeted them at the door with a swinging bicycle chain, sending one of them to the hospital. We all went down the back stairs and fled.

Days later I got up the courage to return. The apartment had been ransacked—by neighbors or cops, who knew which?

Dumped on my closet floor was a boxful of photographs I had made at Antioch when I thought of myself as an artist, pictures strong in texture and tones of gray. Aside from my strewn-around clothes, these were the last personal things I owned. I left them in a heap. I couldn't use them now. There was no space in my life for art. Or nuance.

Reinforcing the separate reality of life in the Machine was the escalating state of confrontation with the cops, not all of which was directly provoked by us. People were routinely followed by plainclothes officers who made no attempt to be surreptitious, pulled over for the slightest real or concocted infraction of traffic rules, illegally searched, and arrested. "I remember at least three or four times that summer when we were raided by the police," Mike told me. "We'd be sitting around in the collective house and they'd just come in, without any warrants, and terrorize us for an hour or so. Once they hung somebody out the window of a third-floor apartment by his heels."

The sexual promiscuity prevalent in the counterculture went rampant with us. In the early period, this was advanced as smashing monogamy. Mike recalled, "There were male leaders who then had access to all the women. It played a role that it does traditionally in sects. It established these men's power, and broke down any private barriers, and removed any retreat a person could have from the scrutiny of the collective." A Chicago friend who was close to us that summer but never joined told me that a member of the Weather Bureau dangled the availability of sex in an attempt to recruit him, saying, "See her? You could fuck her. You could fuck that one, or that one."

People's emotional memories of the sex life inside the Machine vary from the mild to the searing. I suspect that more—straight—men retain the former, more women the latter. Stella recalled that "you were prey. Sex was obligatory. There was no political defense. The correct line was that everyone should have an equal relationship with everyone. It was almost all forced, as opposed to something with an emotional or friendly level. We were in the midst of tearing each other into little bits. But you felt that if you didn't have sex it was a judgment of you, for not being attractive, say. We were so young, most of us. There were still all those late-adolescent doubts that had to do with your sense of yourself as a sexual person."

Doubts about yourself as a sexual person? For me, the program of smashing monogamy engendered a certain smug revenge. I hadn't ever had a steady girlfriend relationship that was any good, for now-obvious reasons. I could function sexually with women, and did try, or pretend, but what I really wanted was a boyfriend, which was an impossibility at least as long as I remained in the closet—or in our organization. I, too, took advantage of the new availability of sex on demand with women. But it was always straight men, my straight friends, dashing leader types typically, whom I really wanted. And with the exception of a fleeting period toward the end of the Machine days, male homosexuality was out of the question in our macho culture. Lesbianism did not quite pose the same threat, a phenomenon akin to the titillation of girl-on-girl sex in the hetero pornography produced for male viewers. Now and then I would proposition one of those guys I desired. None of them was surprised that I sought sex with men—people usually do already know when you finally confess that you're funny that way—but with one exception, which I'll get around to describing, I was always turned down. And usually, I must say, turned down gently. But then these were my actual friends; they may have felt awkward, but to their credit they didn't gratuitously hurt me. I explained myself to them, and to myself, as being bisexual. Maybe there is such a thing as bisexuality, but for me it was always just a cover for being gay, all the way until I finally did come out, long after Weatherman, in 1990, when I was forty-two.

• • •

The first issue of *The Fire Next Time* had been meant to be accessible. The second, published in mid-September, was like the ravings of a person with a fever. The cover reproduced cartoonist Skip Williamson's "Class War Comix," depicting, among other things, a hippie firing a machine gun, a goggle-eyed police chief jerking off at the mention of "Law'n'Order," and a cop having his teeth knocked out by a kung fu strike. Inside, there were paragraphs of type superimposed roughly over photo collages and scattered ranks of vertical stripes representing the cell bars that held political prisoners. Looped and swagged across the pages, worked in as headlines to some articles and as graphic counterpoint on other pages, ran the lyrics of the Stones' "Street Fighting Man." The revolution was a fast dance to a sexy rock tune, or it was a hilarious comic strip—POW! KA-BOOM!—in which the cops take all the blows. We must have thought this would attract people, though. The issue still included, as our newspaper always had, a coupon readers could mail back to request literature or, by enclosing $5, to become a member of SDS.

I wrote a piece for this issue on "revolutionary culture" entitled "Wargasm." In it I celebrated sex, drugs, rock music, fighting, and any old anti-authoritarian thing that kids felt like doing. A few weeks later, in one of the radical publications that routinely arrived in our mail, I found an angry feminist critique of my article. It had been written by my friend from New York SDS, Michele Clark. She was now a member of the groundbreaking Boston women's group Bread and Roses. I didn't understand, because I still thought of myself as a supporter of women's liberation and didn't want to consider how antagonistic to it Weatherman was. I was awfully glad that my nutty article had been unsigned. Years later I spoke with Michele, and asked if she knew I'd written it. "I didn't," she replied, "but it wouldn't have made any difference. At first, Weatherman had a certain appeal. It had that satisfying quality of putting you right with Che. But once I got it about women, and joined Bread and Roses, it didn't matter. During the underground years, I might wonder about you or about Jeff, and worry about how you were. But by then your politics were beside the point."

In Chicago, as the days counted down to October 8 and our National Action, we still had close ties with a local group of leftist lawyers, and with Rising Up Angry, a Chicago organizing project among working class white kids started by some people from SDS. The radical Student Health Organization had agreed—reluctantly—to provide first aid during the demonstrations. But we had succeeded in alienating virtually everybody else. No matter; we knew that the masses of kids were with us. I find that I was cited in the newspaper *Chicago Today*, as late as September 23, asserting that between five and ten thousand of them would be joining us in the streets.

But the reality was that we had isolated ourselves almost completely. This is what happens when you insist you are totally right, belittle everybody else as wrongheaded and "objectively" counter-revolutionary, and deride them all as wimps. We acted as if we didn't care that our ties to the larger movement were being severed. We pretended it proved our superiority. Driven by spite, it seemed easy to cut ourselves off from the rest of the New Left. But it was not so easy to extricate ourselves from our relationship with the Black Panther Party, a relationship that was a swamp of mutual using. The Panthers had come into being on a call for armed self-defense and self-determination for black people, who they defined as constituting an internal colony of the U.S. In many cities they also undertook service work, primarily a free breakfast program for children, which was community building and not incidentally attracted considerable support for their organization.

At an SDS national meeting back in the spring, over objections by the PL camp, SDS had officially declared the Black Panther Party to be the "vanguard" of the revolutionary movement. Three months later, at the SDS convention in Chicago, the Panthers figured significantly in the split with PL. Hoping that it would intimidate the PL delegates, our side arranged for some Panthers to speak. They would do our dirty work for us by denouncing PL for racism—that is, for not having agreed that the Panthers were the vanguard—and for lacking militance. But a Panther speaker, after doing so, went on to praise what must have been his idea of the essence of white counterculture, psychedelic drugs, and free love. He called for women to use "pussy power" to recruit more men. Until that moment, he had been interrupted continually by boos from the PL minions and cheers from the rest of us, but this was way beyond what could be openly stated in SDS, and now widespread jeering and a chant of "Fight Male Chauvinism" made it impossible for him to continue.

A second Panther speaker compounded the problem, repeating the unoriginal quip that "the correct position for women in the movement is prone." Pandemonium ensued, but now we had an excuse for ejecting PL from SDS: their disrespect of these anointed revolutionary leaders. The sexual politics of this incident and our own opportunistic use of it were never afterward addressed in Weatherman—at least not in my hearing. A few weeks later the Panthers held a conference in Oakland to call for building a "United Front Against Fascism." Some Weatherpeople in attendance offered less than wholehearted support of their proposal because, I suppose, we didn't actually want to be part of a mass united front, we just wanted to be the white revolutionary vanguard. Liberation News Service reported that a Panther declared, "We don't see SDS as being so revolutionary. We'll beat those sissies, those little schoolboys' ass if they don't straighten up their politics." This was humiliating, but also bewildering. We had declared them to be leaders of the revolution in part because of their militance, and we were hell-bent on being as militant as possible ourselves. Now they were disparaging us for not signing on to their mass front—and for being cowards, too.

At the N.O. the situation was aggravated by the fact that the Panthers' much poorer Chicago office was just blocks down Madison Street from ours. Weatherman inherited a relationship with the local chapter in which we tried to provide them with what material support we could spare, and they felt justified in taking as much as they could get. Primarily this amounted to our supplying printing, for which they rarely or maybe never reimbursed us. It was hard not to resent this, since we were always short of money for our own projects. At the same time, Panther members were being harassed and busted, and their offices around the country, including the one down the street, were repeatedly assaulted by police, with a degree of lethal violence we never experienced. We continued to publicly adulate the Panthers, and demand that their jailed leaders be released. So it was confusing and dispiriting when they refused to support our National Action. "We don't support people who are anarchistic, chauvinistic, maso- and Custeristic," their Illinois chairman Fred Hampton was quoted in *The Chicago Tribune*. "Revolution and uprising is an art, and we've got to move from that premise. If you persist in these spontaneous acts, we are going to have to look on you as pigs or pig agents." In December 1969, when he was twenty-one, police shot Fred Hampton dead, in his bed with his girlfriend by his side.

But there were mixed messages from the Panthers. Hampton's comment contradicted the concept articulated by Panther co-founder and Minister of Defense Huey Newton, the idea of revolutionary suicide. We liked that one better. In Weatherspeak we had an alternate phrase for the same thing: going out in a blaze of glory. A blaze, at least in my imagining, of bullets.

• • •

Seven white antiwar activists and the Black Panther leader Bobby Seale had been charged under federal law with conspiracy and inciting riot, for having organized the protests during the Democratic Convention the summer before. September 24 was the opening day in their trial. Several thousand people, mostly black high school students, demonstrated at the Federal Courthouse. The Chicago Weather collective charged into the streets, and confronted the police. The next issue of *New Left Notes* reported that "15 people were hospitalized, 10 of them pigs. 18 people were busted....Three of these were arrested at gunpoint in a raid at an apartment several hours later, and four others in the following days." Among those last was Stella, apparently misidentified, since she in fact had not attended the demonstration. The drawn guns of the police convinced the office staff to open the security gate. Stella was dragged down the stairs and out the door by her hair. A Panther spokesman was quoted in the press blaming "stupid, asinine, muddleheaded anarchists" for the violence on September 24. He meant us. Meanwhile, in the courtroom, the judge refused Bobby Seale's request for a postponement because his attorney was ill and unable to attend, and also denied him the right to defend himself. In response to Seale's furious denunciations, on October 29, the judge ordered him bound, gagged, and shackled to his chair.

On October 3, there was another armed police assault on the Panthers' Chicago office. Though we felt undermined by them, we also felt horrified and helpless—and also encouraged in our unproven theory that raising the level of confrontation between white radicals and the state would help relieve pressure on the black movement. We gave a press conference at the spot in Grant Park that had seen the fiercest of the police assaults on demonstrators the year before, to put this idea forth. You can see a video clip from it in various documentaries. Jeff, Bill, and Mark all spoke. Mike and I stood nervously behind them trying to appear hulking, cigarettes dangling from our lips, glaring at the cameras from behind our shades.

The last issue of our newspaper before the National Action had an unambiguous theme of armed revolution, with articles on four Latin American insurgencies. *New Left Notes* had often printed a roundup of short items of movement news. This time, under the headline "Insurrection!" we ticked off several militant street battles of the Weatherman type, and seven recent bombings of National Guard armories and federal buildings in various locations around the country. Weatherman hadn't yet blown anything up, but that idea was in the air. Some people were beating us to it.

• • •

Fearing a police attack during the National Action, we decentralized the office. Stella had been saddled with the appallingly boring job of keeping our books; SDS had been audited a year or two earlier by the Internal Revenue Service, in a move meant to uncover our funding sources and harass us. It seems odd now that after the Weatherman coup we even bothered with bookkeeping, the point of which would have been to keep us out of legal trouble; the threat of jail never stopped us from smashing in storefronts or lobbing rocks at the cops. In the end, Stella's labors were pointless, since we abandoned the N.O. and let SDS collapse before it was time to file another tax return the following spring.

She spent the days of the National Action hiding out with the boxes full of financial records at the apartment of somebody's friend who was not publicly linked to us. The membership files were stashed somewhere else. Communications during the National Action were handled over the phone at another supporter's home—with the various leaders calling in from pay phones to leave and pick up messages. Since we knew arrests would be inevitable, a bail operation was set up in advance, in a room at a Holiday Inn. Our biggest tangible assets, and the most unwieldy, were in the print shop. Moving the unwieldy photography equipment and two heavy presses was out of the question. But even if they were destroyed, we would still be able to publish using outside printers, as long as the typesetting machines—three consoles, each the size of a small desk—and the tools used in paste-up could find a new home.

That was three rooms in a small office building at the corner of Clark and Diversey, just north of Lincoln Park, near the lakefront. This was a different world from the derelict Near West Side block of Madison Avenue where the N.O. was located. It was a tidy neighborhood of hotels and apartment houses, shops and restaurants—and gay people. The adjacent gay neighborhood that later became known as Boystown is a bit north of there, but in 1969 this very corner was the center of visible gay life, such as it was. I posed, to the rental agent, as a publication designer, and leased the space under the name Future-A-Graphics. A select few others knew about this office, but at first I was the main person who spent time there. There was carpeting on the floor. I bought a second-hand couch. From somewhere came a record player and a stack of LPs. The place was quiet, and because it was secret, it felt safe.

These sound like meager comforts, but compared to how we'd been living they felt like luxuries. Coming into possession of this space at the precise moment when most of my comrades were facing an, er, Custeristic street fight, one might expect that I felt a renewed guilt at my privileged place in the organization. In fact, I felt more focused and purposeful setting up this clandestine propaganda office and running it through and after the National Action than I had at any time since coming to Chicago. As always, I found the secrecy satisfying. It seemed to put me apart from, and above, other people, Weatherpeople and strangers alike. And the relative comfort here seemed to promise that clandestine work came with fringe benefits, for example this safe and private space where I not only worked but in effect lived.

Still, every time I emerged onto the street, or went downstairs to the diner for a bowl of soup, I felt unnerved by the vista of a gay community more visible and, though tentatively, more self-confident than any I had ever seen. I lived to regret the name Future-A-Graphics, too. After the National Action, due to our sloppiness, the secrecy of this office was blown, and it became just another place for essentially homeless Weatherpeople to hang out. Others who came there noticed the local subculture, too, and Future-A-Graphics was quickly shortened to FAG, or the fag office. This seemed uncomfortably aimed at me, although I called it that, too. And I was only half-joking, in a conversation there one day about scams we might pull to get some cash, when I suggested that we "go downstairs and roll some faggot."

• • •

On Sunday, October 5, 1969, as if to remind us why we were doing all this, John Soto, a sixteen-year-old resident of an all-black West Side public housing project, was shot to death by a Chicago cop. Life before the cell phone camera: This murder rated a two-inch item on page five of the next day's *Tribune*. But it received more attention a few days later—front page, above the fold—after his older brother Michael, on leave from the army to attend the funeral, was also killed by police "when they turned fire on him as they chased him from a robbery attempt." Or so the story was reported.

Early on Monday, October 6, in Chicago's Haymarket Square, an explosive device partially destroyed a statue of a cop that had been erected to commemorate a policeman killed there by an anarchist's bomb in 1886. It was at this site that we planned to conclude, on the following Saturday, our four days of kick-ass demonstrations. I was asleep on the couch at Future-A-Graphics that Monday morning when I was awakened by a phone call from Bill Ayers, asking me to meet him right away at the N.O. Bill instructed me to call a press conference. "Tell them we don't know who did it, or anything about it, but that it proves how much the people of this city hate the police." It is a measure of my total immersion in the group psychosis of Weatherman that I not only enthusiastically carried out this order but also accepted Bill's disclaimer at face value and remained convinced of its truth for years. Responding to what I told the press, the head of the Chicago Police Sergeants' Association was quoted in the following day's papers saying, "SDS has declared war on the Chicago police. From here on in, it's kill or be killed."

Not all the provocations were coming from our side, and neither was I the only gullible player. In 1989, I spent some days at the

Chicago Historical Society, picking through the files they inherited from the Chicago Police "Red Squad," a group of detectives focused on us and other leftists. Reported deadpan—and taken seriously, one assumes with a flicker of anxiety for the escalation, or retaliation, they might have elicited—are a series of entries that by their improbability and crudeness must be the work of other cops, most likely the FBI's Counterintelligence Program. An anonymous phone tip on the evening of October 7 described plans being made to "conduct a violent demonstration at the United States Armed Forces Examining Station....Weapons, hand grenades and dynamite is to be used." Under the title, "Hippies, and Assassination of Mayor Daley," another anonymous phone call was logged on the afternoon of October 8. The speaker declared that he and four other males, "all Hippies...had made a pickup of Narcotics and Guns and Ammunition....Most of their conversation was that they were going to assinate [sic] Mayor Daley on the Last day of the [conspiracy] Trials, and that it would be an all out effort." Also on October 8, just hours before the start of our National Action, a car parked in a police parking lot had its windshield bashed and a note stuck under a wiper on which was scrawled "WE WILL GET ALL YOU PIG MOTHER FUCKERS/DEATH TO PIGS/POWER TO THE PEOPLE & SDS." That one might actually have been ours.

After dark that evening I walked from the new propaganda office the few blocks to the spot in Lincoln Park where the pitiful Weather army was gathering. It was chilly. A bonfire had been lit, and a few people were busting up a wooden bench for fuel. I hung back, at the edge of the gathering, feeling out of it and ambivalent.

Almost nobody acknowledged me. I certainly was not recognizable to all the members of the city collectives, who comprised the majority of people there. Also, because I was not wearing a helmet like most of them, nor like many carrying a sign affixed to a length of two-by-two which would later see duty as a club, perhaps I was mistaken for a plainclothes cop, which is what the other shadowy figures lurking on the periphery probably were. Or maybe speaking to me, uttering any inessential syllable at all, might have been too painful to those clenched jaws, might have prompted the collapse of those girded shoulders: The fear was palpable. The army of radicalized greasers, the trainload of thousands from Detroit, the charging masses of revolutionary youth, had not shown up. Only the Weather Machine—whose total membership probably did not reach 250—and a smattering of friends and supporters. These dispirited warriors milled about as latecomers straggled in across the lawn. In all, there were perhaps four hundred people.

When the group took off out of the park, I tagged along at a distance, turning back when the missiles started flying and I heard the first shattering glass and sirens. I walked briskly back to the sanctuary of my office and waited to hear about it on the radio. For me, this screaming climax to all we had done since June was muffled and dreamy, like an out-of-body experience. I went through those next days essentially alone, on my connected but singular trajectory.

My assignments for the National Action were to publish a wall newspaper that our troops could plaster up around town, to be our spokesman to the media, to handle whatever unexpected crises arose, and above all, to not get busted so I could do those things.

Thus my own paralyzing fear of fighting the cops was rendered officially irrelevant, my desire to avoid confrontation sanctioned. To accomplish all this, in addition to the propaganda office to hide in, I had: the phone numbers of our secret communications center, the motel room from which bail money would be raised, and the church basements where most of our people were staying; not one but two cars, both previously unassociated with us, a rented lime green Nova coupe and a Mustang fastback requisitioned from somebody's uninvolved former boyfriend; and stashed in my right boot, $3,000 in fifties and hundreds, the equivalent of around $20,000 in 2016 dollars. I was for all practical purposes underground during those days. And I felt at home in that notional space. Secrecy equaled safety. Hiding came naturally to me.

• • •

On that Wednesday night, the Weathertroops charged out of Lincoln Park and started trashing cars and breaking windows in the classy Gold Coast neighborhood, but the mob was split up by police counterattacks. Several people were hit when cops drove right into the crowd, and ten demonstrators were wounded when police fired shotguns. Sixty-three were arrested. On Thursday morning, about fifty members of a Weather "women's militia" tried to march on the Armed Forces Induction Center. Within minutes of stepping off, twelve of the leaders were arrested. The rest, forced to relinquish the clubs, sections of pipe, and lengths of chain they were armed with and to remove their helmets, were escorted by police to a subway station. Meanwhile, the governor called up nearly 2,700 National Guardsmen. They were stationed at high schools where we had announced that on Friday we would stage "jailbreak" actions, running through the halls exhorting kids to walk out, and haranguing classes as had been done at the community college in Detroit.

On Thursday at noon, accompanied by trusty Willett for protection, I gave a press conference outdoors in the Civic Center plaza. I have viewed a videotape of this in which I appear frightened and stiff, and no wonder. The plaza is fronted by Chicago City Hall and a county court building, and was crowded with angry government workers on their lunch hour—possibly the worst place in the city to have chosen. I was threatened and heckled as I read jerkily from my notes. I occasionally gave the cameras a hostile glance. "The ruling class in their Gold Coast decadence will walk the streets a little less secure tonight. If they hadn't dug it before, they'd better dig it now: they are the enemy," I pronounced. And, "The schools are prisons in which the white supremacist ideology of imperialism is forced on kids through the lying racist curricula." And other similar flights of jargon and bluster. I refused to take questions, and then Willett and I were chased down into the subway before squeezing to safety behind the closing doors of a train.

Back at FAG, I wrote and pasted up a wall newspaper and took it to the N.O. to be printed and then delivered to the church basements where the Weathertroops were billeted—we called those places "movement centers," which seems rather grandiose since we hadn't fomented a movement. I think a few people may have gone out pasting up those posters, but I've never seen an archival copy after the fact, not even among the Red Squad papers, which contain an otherwise remarkable collection of Weather ephemera. After Wednesday night's debacle, morale was in the pits. It dropped further when the cops thwarted the women's march on Thursday. Some people joined a protest Thursday afternoon outside the conspiracy trial, which was part of a parallel but non-confrontational series of demonstrations that same week organized by our now-despised former comrades in RYM II. The Weatherpeople who attended had to endure the humiliation of hearing Fred Hampton, the chairman of the Illinois Panthers, declare, "We do not believe in premature so-called acts of revolution. We support the actions of RYM II and no other faction of SDS."

From time to time, members of the Weather Bureau would show up at the movement centers to exhort the dispirited troops, and then retreat again to the safe houses where they were holed up. On Thursday night, some people voiced criticisms of them for not discussing street tactics for Wednesday's action in advance and for allowing that march to be split up. The leaders then turned around to accuse their underlings of blind obedience to discipline and leadership. Criticism by the leaders of the members for following the leaders' leadership is the sort of mental contortion that you might expect would prompt some people to quietly gather their belongings and head for the nearest exit. According to the report of a police informer, it had a different effect on members of the Chicago collective, who proceeded to brainstorm what to do on Friday in place of the high school jailbreak, which was now canceled in light of the presence of the National Guard. Their ideas allegedly included plugging the exhaust pipes of police cars by shoving potatoes onto them to cause their engines to fail, and filling bottles with buckshot and cherry bombs, lighting the firecrackers' fuses, and tossing the missiles through the open windows of police cars. More evidence of clear thinking: This reportedly animated discussion took place between 3:30 and 5:00 a.m.

On Friday afternoon, at one of the movement centers, a plainclothes cop was recognized. He was taken into a room and, in the words of someone who was present, "beaten to a pulp." That night, a big meeting was held to psych people up for the final march on Saturday. The meeting was raided by about 120 policemen who had warrants for the arrest of six people for doing the beating. A few people escaped but the rest were forced to stand around the perimeter of the room, while thirty-eight more were fingered as having been involved in the fighting on the Gold Coast and carted off to jail.

Liberation News Service reported that many demonstrators expected that people would die during the final march on Saturday at Haymarket Square. "If you go back to your home," one was quoted, "and you've had your arm shot off, or your best friend has been killed—let's consider the possibilities—but if this happens and you still want to fight, that's going to impress the hell out of them." In the event, it wasn't much of a demonstration. Even before it got under way, five of the identifiable leaders were arrested. After parading a few blocks along the agreed-upon route, the marchers broke in another direction, but were quickly overwhelmed by the huge police presence. Little "material damage" was achieved but casualties were heavy. Some thirty policemen were injured, one having been thrown through a plate glass window, and Chicago's assistant corporation counsel Richard Elrod, diving to grab a demonstrator, hit a wall instead and broke his neck. More than 180 demonstrators were busted that day. The number of people arrested in the four days, some multiple times, was around 250, just about the entire Weather Machine, plus a few hapless hangers on.

• • •

As I have said, I was not present for most of these events, and neither was I injured or arrested. But I did have my own unnerving related experience. I got a call late on the Friday night from one of the people who had been left to guard the N.O., speaking from a pay phone a few blocks away from there. They had received a frantic call from a kid who was a contact of the Chicago collective—a contact at that point being somebody who was still willing at all to talk to us. He had agreed to store a valise at his parents' house, not knowing what was in it. The parents had found it and discovered that it contained handguns. They were threatening to call the cops unless we retrieved it at once.

I headed for their western suburb on the Eisenhower Expressway. It was dark and drizzling. The Mustang was a fast car and I turned it loose. I was a reckless driver then. I had been up all the night before, putting the wall newspaper together, so I may have drowsed off. Suddenly, blinking barricades appeared in front of me and I skidded to a stop on the shoulder. My first bleary thoughts were that the phone call to my office had been tapped, or that the Mustang was not as anonymous a car as we'd thought. I assumed that this was a roadblock set up to capture me and that I was on the way to jail for illegal possession of firearms—though I didn't have them in my possession yet. Actually, there had been a wreck and one lane of the highway was closed. The cop who shined his flashlight in my face warned me in an avuncular tone to slow down, since it was raining.

I arrived in the middle of a shouting match between our frightened contact and his freaked-out parents, in their paneled recreation room. I backed out of there right away, with the valise of weapons. I couldn't think where else to hide them other than in the trunk of the Mustang, which I left parked on a residential street not far from my office for the next few days. So the utility of having two cars at my disposal was demonstrated. This gave me a sense of what it is nowadays fashionable to call "agency," the power to make a decision and carry it out. But that was a mirage if the context—our failed strategy and decimated organization—is kept in mind. Those two cars, and all that cash in my boot, et cetera, also reinforced my illusion that clandestine work would somehow naturally furnish plentiful resources, and a dark glamour. I was starring in my own movie.

It was right in the middle of those feverish Days of Rage, Jeff told me when I saw him years later, that the Weather Bureau made the decision to transform the visible Weather Machine into an invisible underground. Perspective and composure were apparently not deemed essential for the taking of such a momentous decision. But we had gone far out on a limb and discovered that everybody else was ready to leave us dangling there, so I think we all felt that we might as well jump; it certainly wouldn't do to wimp out on our commitment to ceaseless escalation. There is also the reading of this decision as an adolescent tantrum: If we were to die in the act of committing revolutionary suicide, it would serve everybody else right. And there is the psychological reading, in which it isn't a surprise that the leadership made the decision to go underground when they did. What a spectacular way to repair their punctured collective self-esteem, given the colossal defeat they had ushered us to.

Actually we were already primed and practicing for clandestinity. The informant who described those Chicago collective comrades brainstorming at the movement center how to attack policemen also reported that on the same day some of them were busy changing their appearances by getting their hair cut and dyed, shaving beards, and buying outfits of conventional clothing. The person who beat that other undercover cop to a pulp was not in fact arrested in the raid on the movement center that it provoked; he had already been hustled away—I presume to a safe house set up for such a need—and was, from that very afternoon, the first Weatherperson to go underground, not surfacing again in his own identity for years. The Weather Bureau had already been holding its meetings clandestinely. We had begun to acquire guns and, it is now obvious to me in reconsidering the bombing of the Haymarket Square statue, explosives. As things worked out, it would be another five months before the organization finally vanished from sight. Although for a moment or two, to me at least, the salvation of secrecy seemed to have arrived.

It was on Sunday, October 12, that my marching orders arrived. I was to go to ground in a supporter's secure apartment, do something to alter how I looked, and wait for further instructions, while cataloguing everything I knew about the operation of the National Office. It might seem a security risk to write all of that down, but there would have been chaos if I disappeared with it all in my head. And the leaders weren't really thinking clearly about how and when we would go underground. So there are five pages of remarkably thorough notes in my handwriting, taken from the pocket of an N.O. comrade when he was busted the following day, which I came upon in the Red Squad files. The notes include a floor plan of Future-A-Graphics and a list of publication tasks mundane and grand: "Make some decisions (with WB if you can find them) about whether there's any of last yr's lit to be reprinted...but don't order paper unless you are sure we have stuff to print or it'll be ripoff city." That was a reference to the Panthers' inevitable extortion of free printing if they found we had supplies on hand. I indicated which people knew where various things had been hidden during the National Action. I told the location of five of our cars, who had driven them last, and where their keys might be, noting of the white Dodge that somebody "called early last wk to say that the windshield had been trashed—it is parked on some side street somewhere in the third world...do it soon or it will get towed!"

Some of the notes are cryptic: "Chipmonk shd continue his old Moxie and we want to divide a 500-thing." I can't say for sure but my gut tells me that this last was actually an order for marijuana, to be paid for with organizational funds but enjoyed by the leadership; if so, it wouldn't have been the first or last example of a kleptocratic internal class system. I signed sixteen checks, figuring I guess that this would suffice until somebody else could be made a signatory on the bank account. And I said, "env. in safe with about $700 in it. This is money to use outside of SDS books, for emergencies, freakouts, etc." I took great satisfaction in writing what I thought at the time was a valedictory, and again reading it in the archive twenty years later for its thoroughness and demonstration of my competence. In writing those notes, I was relieved to think that I was marking the end of the stress and discomfort that had pervaded my time at the N.O. I did not expect ever to return there. If the Weather Bureau was blithe in deciding to go underground, I was just as heedless in my eagerness to fabricate a new identity, which is to say to obliterate my real one.

• • •

Yesterday, September 23, 2016, I made an unexpected trip to Chevy Chase for a funeral. Claire Dratch, whom I believe was the last survivor of the group that in 1947 founded the synagogue I attended as a kid, had died at ninety-six. Among the larger group of those founders were four couples, including my parents, who by the time I was born the following year were already very close friends. All eight had left the places where they grew up and come to Washington as adults. A few had relatives nearby, but these four couples forged what we would now call a family of choice. The women, especially, were like sisters, on the phone or in each other's kitchens every day. Coffee was brewed in percolators and consumed around Formica dinette sets by the gallon. The four couples called themselves the New Year's Club, because they went out on the town together every December 31. We had our Passover seders and Thanksgiving dinners and July 4 barbecues with the families of the Club. When we were little, each set of kids called all the other grownups "aunt" and "uncle." Like my parents, the Dratches had three boys and a girl. My sister Marcia is the oldest and their sister Gail the youngest, but we six boys were closely paired off in age, and were three pairs of best friends into our teen years. The Dratches lived about five blocks or ten minutes' walk from us. Closer if you cut through backyards. Faster if you rode your bike.

The synagogue our parents helped established in 1947 and called the Montgomery County Jewish Community Center has a Hebrew name now. The building has been expanded and glamorized, but it is recognizable. When I arrived for Claire's funeral yesterday, there was a preschool class going on in the same room where I went to preschool. This was where I attended summer day camp, and Hebrew school, and Shabbat services, and the bar mitzvahs of my pals. When we Lerners returned from Taiwan in 1959, my father gave a talk at a Friday night service about our exotic life overseas, quoting from vivid letters my mother had sent home that Claire and the other "aunts" had saved for us because they knew the value of memory. Because they did, those letters are the only direct touch I have now with my mother. The sanctuary was packed that night with people whom, at age eleven, I knew by sight if not always by name. The building sits on Freyman Drive, named for Meyer Freyman, the congregation's first president. My father, Abe Lerner, was the second. Their sons, Jeffrey Freyman and Jonathan Lerner, had their bar mitzvah together there one Saturday morning in 1961.

Around the time my mother died, when I was a senior in high school—and largely because she died, which seemed to prove that there was no god—I turned away from Judaism as a religion, and also began to turn away from my family, and our family friends. Yesterday it had been more than fifty years since I stepped foot into that building, which was rightly conceived and named as a community center. I have rarely been back to Washington since I left for Chicago and Weatherman in 1969. My family is long gone, too. But my sister and brothers have kept in contact with the Dratches and our other earliest friends more often than I. They have made a point of it. Me, not so much. I could probably tick off my encounters with them all, since becoming an adult, on ten fingers.

Some of those friends never left Washington, or else returned after college. Some remain members of that congregation. David Dratch, my boyhood bestie, still runs the elegant women's clothing shop his parents opened in 1947. There is a matrix of connection among these people—their children, now, I should say—that still exists, and into which I was welcomed back yesterday immediately and with love. So what made me so ready, and so incautiously eager, to leave it? Why have I had so little hesitation or regret, throughout my life, about giving up people and place and identity, and starting over? I have done so repeatedly. I have moved many times, from places where I had good friends with whom I afterward kept only minimal connection or none at all. I have left one career for another with hardly a backward glance.

From one perspective, this might be evidence of resilience, and I am certainly good at landing on my feet. But it is my highly developed skills at severance that trouble me. What is their source? The profound interruption of living in Taipei for two years as a kid, or the profoundly differentiating condition of knowing I was gay from very early childhood when that was considered a pathology, or possibly the profoundly shattering experience of losing my mother at sixteen? Or did all of these experiences of rupture layered together make me so able, and willing, to relinquish and negate connection? Did doing so in order to be a Weatherman make it more likely that I would replicate the behavior so many times since? Because even amid the bedlam of

1969, it would not have been necessary for me to reject my origins and invent a masked persona just to remain a committed activist against racism and the Vietnam War.

• • •

I spent the few days immediately after the National Action, hair dyed black and dressed in new clothes, floating around Chicago with Jeff, Bill Ayers, and Bernardine Dohrn, in a big wallowy rented Plymouth sedan. What were we doing? We ate in diners—soothing things like rice pudding and scrambled eggs, breakfast food, nursery food; I felt like a child on a holiday. Probably we were living off that cash in my boot. There were things they had to discuss that I couldn't know, so sometimes I would get out of the car, or wait alone for them in it. We all sang along to Elvis Presley's hit of the moment ("We're caught in a trap...") whenever it came on the radio.

I was delegated to find and rent an apartment in a neighborhood where we weren't known. For cover, I decided to say I was an artist who lived in Wisconsin, with inherited money that I wanted to use for a city pied-a-terre so I could drop in to be near the galleries and promote my career. This was easy to pretend to, since something not unlike it could have been my real circumstances if I hadn't taken that hard left turn into radicalism. On a chilly gray day with splatters of rain and drifts of leaves on the sidewalks, a day to evoke a craving for shelter, I headed to the Gold Coast, the place we had attacked just a few days earlier. It was the sort of place my Chevy Chase upbringing might have logically led me to if I had followed a conventional life trajectory. It was the sort of place where I still instinctively felt at home. I inspected charming flats in converted town houses, ultra-modern studios in glass high-rises, places with gleaming wood floors and places with soft carpeting. Inside these refuges, all was serenity and tastefulness. I enjoyed inspecting them, because I expected that I would be living in one of them. One man showed me through his own apartment, which he wanted to sublet. It was filled with antique prints, richly upholstered furniture, oriental rugs, masses of flowers—decor. He was fortyish, well-dressed, and obviously homosexual. In the bedroom, he sat and patted the bedspread, looking me up and down. I could roll this faggot, I thought. Or I could have sex with him. Which choice would reveal a more frightening truth about myself? Short of breath, I made an excuse and fled.

• • •

I suppose it became obvious that the underground need not, or could not, be created in the space of a few days. With deflated spirits, I was sent back to Future-A-Graphics to put out another newspaper presenting our spin on what we had just been through. This issue inaugurated yet another new name, in place of *New Left Notes* or *The Fire Next Time*, simply *FIRE!* It was a single folded tabloid sheet consisting mainly of collaged news photos ripped from mainstream papers—cops bleeding from the head, smashed windows and trashed cars, fights in progress—and fragments from their headlines, like "bloody melee" and "rampage." The centerfold was meant to be used as a poster. Screened over it in red, yellow, and blue was the flag of the Vietnamese National Liberation Front. In the center, surrounded by battle images from the National Action, was a short, strident declaration of victory that I ended with a reference to that police spokesman's reaction to my press conference after the bombing of the Haymarket statue: "DID THAT PIG SAY KILL...OR BE KILLED?" Above it all, in big, blocky 56-point type was our answer. "YOU DON'T NEED A WEATHERMAN TO KNOW." I felt exceedingly clever for creating this piece of literature, if it can be called that, for devising its convention-busting format, and for expressing with it so accurately our attitude that even at that moment of defeat remained blustering self-delusion. We could not admit that we had been wrong about how to mobilize large numbers of young people, nor reveal own our embarrassment and shame at the debacle of the Days of Rage.

Though we weren't blessed immediately with the release that disappearing from public view seemed to promise, things did ease up in some ways. Partly this was due to external circumstances. So many of our people were now facing charges that we at the N.O. became for the next few months largely a legal defense organization. Besides, it was turning cold. Venues for our al fresco style of surprise-attack activism were no longer thronged with young people to assail. And partly the new mood came from within. People were exhausted and bruised. The previously always open question of whether someone—anyone, oneself—was worthy or should be offed was no longer so dominant, as if just surviving through the Days of Rage furnished adequate proof of commitment and zeal. We didn't try to understand our mistakes but we did grasp that something had been not quite right. We still inhabited our own bizarre reality, but it became a bit more benign. "We were on a death trip," was the handy if specious formulation, "and now we're on a life trip." We were no longer deliberately putting ourselves in potentially injurious or suicidal situations. Evenings were a little more likely to be spent drinking or getting high or even doing laundry, less so in criticism/self-criticism marathons.

There were several formal reorganizations through the fall, when the Weather Bureau would return from a secret meeting and announce the closing down of some collective, the shuffling of members from city to city. Several people were sent to work with me as a propaganda collective. I rented a little house for this group to live in, but it soon became just another Weather crash pad. It could sit empty for days—we were as likely to fall asleep on the floor at the office or wherever else in the city we found ourselves, as to return to that house. It was hardly a house, really, just the upstairs of a garage on a back alley, rude and grim as the Chicago workers' housing depicted in Upton Sinclair's *The Jungle*. A steep outdoor flight of wooden stairs led to our first floor, two bare rooms and a bathroom. Another stairway twisted up to an attic where we laid down the usual carpeting of mattresses. The only thing indicating which room was meant to be the kitchen was a little cast-iron gas burner that sat off the floor on eight-inch legs. To heat up a pan of canned beans you crouched down over the thing as if it were a campfire.

I rented this place because it was cheap and walking distance from Future-A-Graphics, and it felt appropriate for a cabal of hooligan revolutionaries hatching plots, with the flickers of that gas ring dancing off our foreheads. I went by that house when I was in Chicago years later. It had been fashionably renovated and its neighborhood is now quite tony, but in late 1969 it was the venue for Weather extremes of all sorts. Stella remembered, for example, being sick there, unnoticed and unaided for days until it occurred to someone to get her to a doctor, who diagnosed pneumonia. Somebody else recuperated there from two miscarriages—or three, but can that be possible?—in as many months. Every few weeks there was a mass court date, when Weather cadres from the various city collectives would converge on Chicago, and on those nights the place might accommodate forty or fifty people. On those evenings, in that house, blow-out parties were held, with people so intent on forcing a good time that some threw up. And it was on that sea of mattresses upstairs that we had several of our infamous orgies.

The crazy collective sex life was in this period, if anything, more pervasive. The counterculture's free love, such as it was, was embraced as a signature feature of our so-called life trip. It went on in that "accidental" way of people who were sharing a mattress falling into sex. There were, despite the still-official position against monogamy, various couples who managed to pair off in this period. Men in leadership continued to pressure women into sex when they felt like it. And sometimes there was an orgy, a more or less command performance. At least one of those was made even weirder by everybody dropping LSD, handed around by me and Bill, some eagerly and some I'm sure feeling pressured into taking that risk, too. People participated in these group sex events with a range of individual agendas. Some hung around the edges just hoping they didn't have to really get involved. Some seized the opportunity to fuck somebody in particular or a lot of people in relatively anonymous succession. Women and men both used them as cover for trying out homosexual connections. I participated—actually, I was one of the instigators. But the truth was that there was one person in particular, not a group, with whom I wanted to make love. I soon got my wish.

Bill Ayers was brash, sweet, irrepressibly charming—to his friends, he was not an armor-plated heavy. He was a proponent of the "life trip" and the accoutrements of hippiedom; he wore a colorful headband to hold back his blond curls. We spent a lot of time together in the months following the Days of Rage. Our conversations grew intimate. We maneuvered into position, as it were, revealing to each other unsatisfactory past experiences we had each had of sex with men. During one of those conversations, at maybe 2 a.m. in an all-night diner in the Loop, a young man came in the door with a pistol in his hand and held the place up for the cash in the till. We watched the stickup unfold with amazement, and afterward marveled at how simple it had been to carry out.

Bill and I said we loved each other, because we did. I don't know him any longer, though I'm pretty sure he's not gay or even in practice bisexual. But in those days we were toppling so many other barriers that making love with me probably seemed to him like just another one to knock down. I think that for Bill, sex with a man was simply one more transgressive thing he would consider trying at least once, like pulling off an armed robbery of a diner, or parachuting from an airplane, or shooting smack, or sticking it to his prominent Chicago family by shipping out on a merchant freighter or by becoming a firebrand revolutionary.

When we did finally go to bed together a few times, no doubt it held more meaning for me; my expectations were greater, and therefore my disappointment. The sex wasn't very good. Neither of us was familiar with or adept at how it goes between men; I learned all that later. But this was the first time I had ever tried it with a guy I knew and loved, eyes open, talking about it together rather than pretending it wasn't happening. I would have wanted to go on and on. I expected making love to instantly transform our friendship into something else. Bill didn't. The few occasions we were together in that way were chosen and delimited by him. He could get away with that via the usual rationales—his leadership responsibilities, pressing revolutionary commitments, demands on him I couldn't know about.

Looked at one way, the whole thing was pretty tawdry. Despite the fumbling mediocrity of the sex and the discordance of its meaning to the two of us, we both boasted widely about having done it, and were awarded a certain amount of awed respect within the organization for our adventurousness. On the other hand, our flaunting of it created, or amplified, a brief opening for the consideration of homosexuality in Weatherman. That might, at the least, have given other closeted people a tiny bit of breathing space. And it prompted some of the straight ones to think about the possibilities. One Weatherman mentioned in an article written during this period "a very heavy discussion we had in N.Y. in which we concluded that it was our male chauvinism alone that prevented us from digging physical contact with other men, and that, if only from a survival standpoint, we should learn to gratify some of our sensuous needs with men as well as with women. (How else are we going to survive long jail sentences?)" Another told me, years later, about a time he was driving somewhere with Mark Rudd. Mark was rambling on about this temporarily fashionable idea that men should learn to be sexual with each other. As often happened in those days, those two ended up sharing a bed that night. "Oh god," this guy remembered thinking. "Am I going to wake up with Mark all over me?" Still, when he later made a trip back to his college, he engaged his best friend there in a conversation about whether they should try becoming lovers.

One other salient fact about our collective sex life in those late months of the Weather Machine: Venereal disease was rampant. People were constantly infesting each other with crab lice. Gonorrhea was passed around, and—more debilitating—some women contracted pelvic inflammatory disease. If this had been a decade later, we would also quite probably have been giving each other hepatitis and HIV, both of which are potentially fatal. No matter; we were working up other ways to kill ourselves.

• • •

You might wonder what we were doing for money. That cash in my boot didn't last forever, and even Cream of Wheat wasn't free. Of course none of us had a job. The influx of SDS membership dues that would normally have arrived in the fall, when colleges resumed, didn't come, because we no longer treated SDS as a membership organization. Money we received from individual donors, a cohort that was rapidly vanishing, mostly went to bailing people out of jail, and perhaps to paying for those rental cars and places like National Forest cabins where the Weather Bureau hid out for their meetings, which offered anonymity but weren't free. So we had to be resourceful.

At least once, we tried extortion. During a huge national antiwar mobilization in Washington that November, Bill and I and a couple of others presented ourselves at the Moratorium office. We were described in *Life* magazine, by a reporter who was in the room, as "flat and grim in their shades and work clothes and heavy boots." We asked for money "with deadpan politeness, a certain delicacy even," in exchange for not disrupting the next day's march. They didn't give us any, and we didn't hold back in the street, but we wouldn't have done so even if they had; we were thieves, rowdies—not diplomats. This was a more audacious attempt than most, but ripping off in thoughtless, mundane ways and in elaborate calculated schemes had become as normal to us as breathing.

A common scam was riffling through drawers in college dorm rooms—in those days, students didn't lock their doors—or stealing purses left unattended, for instance in library carrels. It was winter now; a handbag is easily concealed under a coat. And young, white, longhaired Weatherpeople did not look out of place on a campus. The goal was to find, in addition to money, sets of ID that could be used while carrying out other extra-legal activities. A number of women performed an age-old hustle that didn't require a lot of imagination, in airports or hotels; they would hang around the cocktail lounge until some "businessman" got interested, and then tell a sob story about being broke or having lost a ticket. In a funkier version of this, several former Weatherpeople have told me they had heard, as I had heard myself, "of women in the Detroit collective who raised money by giving hand jobs to truckers for $5." That would amount to about $33 today—quick, dirty, and cheap, but it would buy groceries.

Such low-level but high-risk scams were conducted by people at the base of the organization. The leaders did not make themselves so vulnerable. Available to them were safer, vaguer kinds of theft. People could be seduced, by the intimation of access and reflected celebrity, or by intimidation, into letting themselves be taken advantage of. The victims of this sort of theft were uninvolved old friends and movement people who still thought of us fondly, leftist lawyers who were committed to defending us— people who did not realize or could not bring themselves to acknowledge how destructive, and corrupt, we had become. A car might be borrowed for a day and returned weeks later. Or a house. Bail money might be solicited for the purpose of getting someone in particular out of jail but spent instead to spring someone else deemed more important. Or maybe spent on a white-tablecloth restaurant dinner for the stressed-out leadership.

At least one person went as far as to get married to raise money, to a man in her collective who had perhaps accidentally let on how much it might be worth to his family if he settled down. "It was one of the least principled things that I did," this woman told me, "and the thing I am most ashamed of. He was a very young guy. I didn't even have a sexual relationship with him. We had a wedding, with his family. I stole a dress to wear. His family bought me jewelry. I think they gave us a car, a TV set—but we didn't get all that much loot out of it for the humiliation and pain we caused." Stella remembered being at the home of a lawyer who was working on some of our cases. "I don't think I took anything that time, but I was with someone who did, who looked in his wife's closet and said, 'I like this,' and walked away with it. We hurt the people closest to us. We took from them in every way, materially and emotionally. There was nothing we could offer them back except the glimmer of close proximity. But at the same time we scorned them, for not being with us."

In this shabby behavior Weatherman was operating according to an ethos that was common to the counterculture, at least at its defiantly outlaw frontiers. But as in so much else, we took things further. Among people who had dropped out of conventional society, shoplifting from department and grocery stores was widespread. The use of fraudulent telephone "credit cards" for long distance calls, which were expensive to make in those days, was massive. These weren't cards with a magnetic strip or a chip. They just carried a sequence of letters, the same sequence for all users, which changed but once a year and let you bill calls to your phone number. Or, actually, to any phone number, even a made-up one— such was the rudimentary level of security. I once saw a guerrilla theater troupe spreading the knowhow by performing a little song-and-dance in which the first letter of each word they sang, taken all together, was the long-distance credit card code. "Quick As Ever Harry Jumped Nimbly Right Under Wendy Zimmerman," they chanted while "Harry," bending low, hopped under "Wendy's" upraised leg: QAEHJNRUWZ. Good fun, useful information. In fact, before we took it over, SDS had been threatened with being billed for all the bogus credit card calls the N.O. had received, and *New Left Notes* ran a plea for people to stop making them.

But! But! American Telephone and Telegraph, which at the time had a virtual monopoly on U.S. phone service and was the world's largest corporation, deserved to be ripped off! Corporations, and the ultra-rich, had no right to wealth accumulated in a racist and warmongering economy. There is something to this idea, although it's, well, complicated. But even accepting that rationale, we might have made a distinction between stealing from faceless corporations and ripping off our allies and friends. I don't suggest that every pot-addled shoplifting hippie was as unscrupulous in that way as we were. But it's also true that we were not the only group on the left that had descended to larceny. In fact, of all the incidents of piracy I engaged in or witnessed in the Sixties, the sorriest one without question was when the leadership of the Illinois chapter of the Black Panther Party ripped off the SDS National Office. At gunpoint.

Tensions with the Panthers had escalated after the National Action. They had slandered us in the pig press. We were broken and broke. Ron Fliegelman had recently arrived to run the presses, because of his great mechanical aptitude and because the former printer had fled our craziness. Ron reminded me when I saw him years later that by this time we had decided that we simply couldn't give the Panthers free printing whenever they wanted it.

On the afternoon of Thanksgiving Day, 1969, a group of five or six Panthers, including the chairman, Fred Hampton, arrived at our door in a state of angry agitation. Where was the printing job which we had promised them? (Or, the one that they imagined we had promised them, or felt we should have promised them?) We tried to keep them on the stairs, below the locked gate, while explaining that we couldn't do their printing because we didn't have money to buy paper. Then out came their guns. And open went the gate.

The first target of their wrath was the printer himself, which was unfortunate since in our hierarchy printers were merely skilled drones, not decision makers. One of the intruders asked Ron whether he wasn't a racist for not following the orders of the vanguard party. Ron, a recent recruit but already well indoctrinated, replied something like, "Of course I'm a racist..." and might have gone on to explain how this was inevitable since he was a beneficiary of white skin privilege in a structurally racist society, et cetera. But before he could continue, he was clobbered in the head with the butt of a pistol. While this was going on in the print shop, a couple of the Panthers were ransacking the rest of the office. Then came the demand for cash. None of us had any to speak of, but there sat the safe, as if spotlit. At first we pretended that none of us knew the combination, when in fact Stella and I both had it memorized.

It was the gun to Stella's head, an image still vivid in recollection, which caused me to change tactics and instruct her to open it: She is kneeling at the big iron box, twirling its dial, and the muzzle is lost in her thick hair. There might have been all of $300 or $500 inside, which our visitors pocketed. On the way out, for good measure, they knocked a few other people around, and carried off a fancy typewriter we had on lease from IBM. Nobody was seriously hurt, but four of the N.O. staff did go to an emergency room to get stitched up, where to protect the Panthers and keep the cops out of it they gave a concocted story about having been mugged and beaten on the street. A few days later a delegation from the Weather Bureau—Bernardine, Jeff, and Bill, if I recall—went to the Panthers' office to lodge a protest, and were kicked down the stairs. Behold the toxic ecosystem of sycophancy, bullying, degraded principle, and madness that was our relationship with the Black Panther Party, which some eight months earlier we had declared to be the vanguard of the Amerikkkan revolution.

Like us, they should have had the power to clear their heads and act rationally, and like us, they chose not to do so. But though it is no excuse, it's worth reiterating the context. The Panthers, in Chicago and elsewhere, were on the receiving end of repeated deadly police attacks. Their organization was riddled with provocateurs. Barely a week after our awful encounter with him and his comrades at the N.O., in the early hours of December 4, 1969, Fred Hampton and another Panther, Mark Clark, were shot dead during a police attack on their apartment. Years later it emerged that Hampton had been drugged, and that the cops had been given a floor plan of the apartment indicating the location of his bed, by the same person who had first pointed a gun at us on the N.O. stairs and who then proceeded to pistol-whip Ron Fliegelman and threaten Stella Blank's life. That was a human being by the name of Bill O'Neal. Police operative O'Neal remained for several more years a leading member of the Illinois chapter of the Black Panther Party. After its demise, he committed suicide. Perhaps he can rest in peace.

• • •

It is an indication of the Weather Bureau members' derangement that even as the rhetoric and planning through that autumn of

1969 focused on clandestine, armed action, a brief, half-hearted, and doomed effort to resuscitate SDS as a student-based organization was undertaken. There was discussion about moving the N.O. to Madison, a progressive city where we might face less harassment from the police, and where the University of Wisconsin was one of the strongest bases of radical activism in the country. But we didn't move the office. Two people, Cathy Wilkerson and Teddy Gold, were delegated to be national "campus travelers." Cathy had already been an organizer years before she became the architect and unflagging assembler of what we built in Washington SDS; people used to say she changed their lives. Teddy had been at the center of the Columbia chapter, and of the consequential strike and building occupation there in 1968. Short and nerdy looking, he was quick and brainy, but not intimidating.

But the two most brilliant organizers on earth, even if they had been talking sense, could not possibly have replaced the national apparatus of organizers and chapters that we had already broken apart and dismantled. Even our file of key college contacts had been stolen, in one of the police raids. Still, we published four issues of *FIRE!* between November and January. And as had been the SDS tradition, we held a conference over the New Year holiday. This annual gathering had always been called the National Council. We called ours the National War Council.

The War Council was held in Flint, Michigan, a grim industrial city, not a pleasant college town. The venue was the Giant Ballroom, a dance hall and bowling alley in the city's black ghetto. I was one of the first people to arrive, along with members of my propaganda collective, because we had planned to dress up the hall. We were unable to get started right away because there had been a murder there the night before, and the cops still had it cordoned off; attendees were confronted throughout our gathering by bullet holes in the door and a bloodstain on the floor of the entryway.

I can't claim creative credit for our decorative scheme. On my team was a wild and crazy cartoonist, whose name I don't recall now, who mostly dreamed it up. The story went that members of the New York Weather collective had accosted him one day, in a park, with the usual challenge: "The people of the world are rising up, and you're either with them or against them." Supposedly he immediately replied, "Okay, I'm with them!" and joined up then and there. If this was true, it may have been the only time that this particular organizing approach actually worked. He had the idea to paper the Giant Ballroom's walls, à la Warhol, with a grid of alternating red and black versions of an image of the recently slain Fred Hampton. He made a twenty-foot-long poster covered with drawings of bullets, each labeled with the name of someone we defined as the enemy. That was a category broad enough to include both Chicago Mayor Richard J. Daley and the left-wing weekly newspaper *The Guardian*, which had been critical of our adventures. He also fabricated an enormous cardboard and aluminum-foil mobile in the shape of a machine gun that we suspended from the ceiling. A reporter from Liberation News Service wrote that the ballroom's festoonery "gave it the flavor of a revolutionary cabaret."

There were about four hundred people present. LNS reported that "This was a Weatherman meeting, with a handful of outsiders there to gawk, scowl, listen and occasionally to debate....No specific resolutions were debated or voted on. The only formal structure consisted of speeches by the Weather Bureau." It was a rally, not a conference, all exhortation and no conversation. My most vivid recollection has always been of a moment, during a discussion of smashing monogamy, when some unfortunate fellow spoke up to ask, "What are men supposed to do then, make love with each other?" Bill and I, standing together at the back of the hall, pugnaciously yelled back, "Yeah, exactly, try it, it's outasight," and so forth. But little else stuck in my memory; maybe because it all seemed normal by then—the berserk energy, the manic hilarity, the outrageous assertions—or maybe because I was just sleep deprived.

Liberation News Service's account brought some salient moments back. Teddy was quoted declaring that after an international revolution "an agency of the people of the world" would run the United States, and, "If it will take fascism, we'll have to have fascism." Weather Bureau member John Jacobs gave a talk summarizing the whole of Western history as the "White Devil Theory." Eleanor Stein, who in the underground years was in the top leadership, reminded us of the depiction in *The Battle of Algiers* of women hiding weapons beneath their chadors, and brought the concept home with the suggestion, "Consider the possibilities of the false pregnancy!" The Flint War Council was where Bernardine infamously bragged about walking up the aisle of an airliner taking food off other passengers' trays, and praised the Manson Family's recent ritual murders of wealthy people in Beverly Hills.

The final issue of our newspaper, published a few weeks later, included a poster drawn by that wacky cartoonist showing a long-haired hippie Santa Claus holding a sack of goodies, including rifles, grenades, and dynamite. It read, "Over the holidays we plotted war on Amerika. Ho Ho Ho Chi Minh." A request coupon, like the one that had always been in *New Left Notes*, was included. Instead of the old choices for literature and membership, it simply read—in my own freehand scrawl, I could not help but recognize—"Send me more stuff!" I don't know how many of these order forms may have been returned and then left to drown in the sea of rubbish later abandoned at the N.O. But one resides in the SDS archive in Madison. It was filled in thus: "Abbie Hoffman, c/o Conspiracy Office, 28 E. Jackson Blvd., Chicago, Ill." Abbie had been one of the most visible promoters of the demonstrations at the 1968 Democratic Convention, and was now a defendant in the conspiracy trial. He was one of the creators of the Yippies, or Youth International Party. That was not a real organization but an illusion for the media, and an attitude of absurdist activism for absurd times. Where the form asked for a ZIP code, Abbie altered it to read "YIP."

• • •

In all these months I had escaped being the subject of a criticism/self-criticism. Finally this omission occurred to somebody, and the happy event was scheduled. It took place on the night of one of those mass court appearances, and was eagerly attended by dozens of Weather cadres who were in town from the various collectives. Most of them I knew barely, or not at all. They arrived in a festive mood. I have a vivid image of myself on a stool in the middle of a big circle—as if spotlit, so maybe that is a bit of theatrical confabulation. I guess I was attacked for being a wimp and not kicking butt in the streets, and maybe for individualism at having been solo so much of the time, or for never having previously undergone one of these autos-da-fé—never mind that my job had been to manage the office, not plant Viet Cong flags on beaches, and I hadn't been in a collective. Since I had never learned the script, and the whole exercise made me feel totally undermined, I sat through the excruciating session desperate but almost entirely mute. "Fight for yourself!" a Greek chorus of militiawomen from Detroit kept chanting. When it was over and the disappointed troops were drifting from the room, I noticed that Jeff, my best friend, was asleep in his chair.

There are a number of plausible explanations for this, including that he was embarrassed for me, or that he shut down in denial at the evident stupidity of this supposed cadre-building technique, or maybe he was simply sleep-deprived himself. We didn't discuss it, so I can't say. But I do know that I felt forsaken.

• • •

If there is any sliver of doubt in your mind that Weatherman was trading organizing for terrorism, consider the paths of Cathy Wilkerson and Teddy Gold. A couple of months before Flint, they had been instructed to resuscitate the public mass organization we had recently trashed. But not three months after Flint, in March 1970, they were both members of a collective that was making bombs. These bombs were intended to be set off, for instance, during a dance at an army base where the victims would almost certainly include not only soldiers but also their dates. Instead, one blew up while my comrades were putting them together, in the basement of Cathy's father's Manhattan town house. The building was wrecked. Teddy and two other Weatherpeople, Terry Robbins and Diana Oughton, were killed.

After Flint, but before that disaster, there were further reorganizations, conducted with increased secrecy; it wasn't always made known where someone was being sent. A new self-doubt began to unsettle members of the Weather Machine. Before, we had worried that we would not be fierce enough as street fighters, and perhaps would be offed from the organization because of it. Now we worried that we would not receive what Teddy and I, at least, only half-jokingly called "the tap on the shoulder" inviting us into the underground. Everything Weatherman had said and done in the previous six months led inevitably to the misconception that the only valid and glorious thing to be was a guerrilla fighter. We possessed the National Office and the organization's paltry remaining resources, but over the months since taking power we had bled SDS to death, and dismissed the idea of mass organization altogether. It was obvious now, if you were close enough to the center and paying attention, that a clandestine structure dedicated to armed action was being constructed, and that some individuals were being moved into it. It also became clear that the decisions about who would get to be part of it belonged to the leaders, not to the members. I say "get to be" deliberately. To go underground was a prize, like a special treat for an overexcited child—the extra scoop of ice cream, the second turn on the roller coaster.

When I got my assignment, it was not what I'd hoped for. Instead of heading into a secret cell and the romantic underground life I had expected would be mine, I was sent to Cuba on the Venceremos

Brigade. The Venceremos Brigade had been founded the previous year, during a trip to Cuba by representatives of SDS, to bring groups of young Americans to the island for work projects. For our side, it was a way to demonstrate solidarity with a revolution we idolized. For the Cuban government, it was an investment in propaganda—American kids flaunting the U.S. policy of blockade—since the cost of transporting, housing, feeding, and fêting groups numbering in the hundreds for two-month visits far exceeded the value of our labor. About thirty members of Weatherman were sent on this brigade in February of 1970.

This was a way to neither off us nor tap us on the shoulder. I wasn't asked if I wanted to go to Cuba, or even told how it was decided that I should. Obediently, as usual, I acquiesced. But no amount of rationalization could soften the blow, not the honor of being deputized to maintain our organizational contact with the Cuban government, nor the fiction that our work cutting sugar cane would be a material contribution to their revolution. I wanted to be with my friends in the underground. I wasn't exactly being purged, but it felt like a trip to purgatory.

Along with Sarah Kramer and Christine Jensen, two members whom I barely knew, I was designated as a leader of this contingent. (Sarah and Christine are pseudonyms.) Chaperone a bunch of losers on a frivolous winter sojourn to a tropical island? It made me feel like a loser, too. Meanwhile, it seemed that everyone in the organization to whom I was close—Cathy, Mike, Jeff, Phoebe, Bill, Karin, Naomi, Willett, Teddy—would get to dye their hair and live in secret apartments and make cloak-and-dagger rendezvous to plan spectacular explosions of righteous anger that would shock the world.

That cinematic idea of being underground was my fantasy, of course. It was also my—paranoid—fantasy to perceive that I was being cut loose by the organization. In fact, Mark Rudd, representing the Weather Bureau, showed up at the pier in St. John, New Brunswick, where a Cuban ship had been sent to pick up us *brigadistas*. (It was not possible to travel there directly from the U.S.—we were running the blockade, a fact the Cubans always featured prominently in discussing the Brigade.) He came to see us off, and to make an arrangement for how we should get back in touch when we returned at the end of April. It was generally expected that by then the organization would have disappeared from view. But Mark promised there would be a letter waiting, telling us what to do. Where to send it? Sarah had a cousin in Canada. She wrote the address inside a matchbook. Mark put the matchbook in his pocket. It was snowing, that February afternoon in St. John, as I climbed the gangway onto the Cuban ship. I couldn't know that it would be not in spring, two months hence, but winter and nearly a year later before I would be back again with my Weatherman co-conspirators.

School-issued photo identification card, 1953. "I like to imagine that this was an artifact of Cold War paranoia, given that we were in a Washington suburb and half of our fathers were federal employees. Surely we never had to show these—they just made us feel important. I was in kindergarten, age 5."

Photograph courtesy Jonathan Lerner.

With younger brother Higgy (left) older brother Steve, and unidentified pedicab driver outside No. 6, Lane 85, Sung Jiang Liu, Taipei, where the Lerner family lived 1957-1959. "At first we were shocked by the poverty of Taiwan. But it took very little time for it to seem totally normal that a fellow wearing only cloth slippers on his feet would haul us around town in a pedicab. Taiwan is a rich country now and today this street is probably lined with gleaming highrises."

Photograph courtesy Jonathan Lerner

After winning a Halloween costume contest, Grand Hotel, Taipei, Taiwan, 1958. "I was mortified when I found this forgotten act of appropriation among my parents' things, years later."
Photograph courtesy Jonathan Lerner.

Age 17, at home in Chevy Chase, Maryland, March, 1965. "I guess I'd put aside *The New Yorker* for a minute, to read the funny pages in *The Washington Post*."

Photograph courtesy Jonathan Lerner.

(1) John Lerner   (2) Nick Greer   (3) Gordon C. Folkemer   (4) Fred Barsky

An action to prevent a speech by then-San Francisco Mayor Joseph Alioto, Georgetown University, Washington, D.C., March 13, 1969. "That's me at right, arm raised, number 1. Students at San Francisco State College had been on strike for five months, demanding increased enrollment and faculty positions for people of color, and ethnic studies curricula. Alioto's police were beating them up almost daily."

Photo from the online archives of a House Internal Security Committee investigation of SDS.

sds National Office

SDS, 1608 West Madison, Chicago, Illinois 60612
phone (312) 666-3874

4 September

Dear BL

It was good, though hard, to see you when you were here. I am more and more finding that living and working the way we do makes it a real trip to spend time with people who are not directly & immediately involved in one's scene. It's like time out, or mixing worlds, and it always blows my mind a little bit.

Thanx for the contribution too--we are as usual four million bucks in the hole.

What can I say? Keep on truckin

Love

Jonny

PS You are now a member of sds!

Letter to Barbara Leckie, September 4, 1969. She says, "Given my background as a red diaper baby, if you were trying to foment a revolution, you had a rough road to hoe if I was a challenge." Reprinted with permission of Barbara Leckie.

In Lincoln Park, Chicago, 1972.

Photos by Barbara Leckie, reprinted with permission.

With Colin Neiberger and Jennifer Dohrn, New York City, 1973.
Photo by Bart Lubow, reprinted with permission.

Shortly after the Wounded Knee uprising, Rapid City, South
Dakota, May, 1973.

Photographer unknown.

With Cree acquaintances at James Bay, Quebec, on assignment for *Rolling Stone*, August, 1974. First Nations traditionalists were opposing the construction of a hydroelectric installation that would eventually flood 6,750 square miles of their hunting and fishing grounds. "They lost their fight against the power company. My article was never published, either. I hadn't yet learned how to write a decent—or unbiased—feature story."

Photograph courtesy Jonathan Lerner.

In a tipi at James Bay, Quebec, August, 1974. "I had just returned from a walk in the woods, and was feeling sheepish. My Cree hosts thought I'd got lost in the wilderness and had scattered in all directions looking for me."

Photograph courtesy Jonathan Lerner.

Near Grand Canyon, Arizona, on assignment for *Landscape Architecture Magazine*, May, 2016.

Photograph courtesy Jonathan Lerner.

3.

I missed a lot of iconic movies in those years. Pocket money was short. And a lot of the time we had something more urgent to do, like sitting around in endless stupefying meetings. Also, while it wasn't a formal policy, aside from rock and roll, appreciating culture whether mass or highbrow carried a whiff of bourgeois self-indulgence. I never visited a museum or gallery then, either, or attended a play. Of course, there were exceptions. In the summer of '69, as the Machine was being hammered into existence, many people in Weatherman saw *Butch Cassidy and the Sundance Kid*, which was the source of our glamorization of going down in a "blaze of glory." People used to refer to Bill Ayers and his pal Terry Robbins, who died along with Teddy in the town house explosion, as Butch and Sundance, but I've still never seen the film so I can't say which of them was meant to be whom. I do remember going to the movies that summer once, with Phoebe, to see *Midnight Cowboy*. I found its depiction of gay hustling unsettling, and seductive.

I never saw Bertolucci's 1970 masterpiece *The Conformist*, either, until last night (nor had I read the Alberto Moravia novel it is based on). If I had seen it back then, it would have disturbed me, too, being, as described recently by *The Guardian* (the English daily, not the defunct American leftist weekly), an "account of the neuroses and self-loathing of a sexually confused would-be fascist," who joins Mussolini's secret police. Fascism, communism—as ethical systems or utopian visions they differ considerably. But in actual history, the political structures that have arisen to support them are equivalent, in the sense that both can provide the opportunity to submerge homosexual panic in the appearance of normalcy and, even better, in secret work and, better still, secret work with the promise of violence. *The Conformist*'s depiction of homosexual panic as a motivation, in particular, resonates with me. But don't get the idea that I'm beating up on gay people; any number of confusions, insecurities, and pathologies can move people to deny their individuality and abdicate their responsibilities and critical faculties in order to join a hierarchy or cult, political or otherwise. No doubt my leftist loyalty would have prevented me from making this observation when the film was released in 1970, so it's just as well I didn't see it then.

Last night I noted yet another truth in *The Conformist*: Even within an organization where membership requires adherence to an ideology and surrender of individuality, the common experience and the particular experience always coexist. While marching forward, everyone remains an individual on a unique path. My route through the Weather Machine was atypical—I was not in a collective, not obliged to fight, not busted on felony charges, and I enjoyed unusual proximity to the power center of our hermetic little world. But the story any Weather person could tell would differ from every other. Headed for Cuba I was still, as I might have phrased it then had it occurred to me to remark it, on my own trip. And for me the year that began when I was directed to go there was even more conspicuously singular than what had come before, or would come later.

Sarah, Christine, and I got right to work, pretty much ignoring our Weather underlings—probably to their relief—and demanded a meeting with the Cuban officials on board the ship. They had been following developments in our movement, and were bemused by the phenomenon of Weatherman, but since we were inheritors of the history of contact between SDS and them, they were willing to talk with us. They failed to grasp, we explained, the central role of black nationalism in the U.S. struggle, and they should set up separate work and living groups for the black members of the Brigade. Well, they replied, conditions were different in the States but Cuba was a multiracial society where everybody worked together. Why didn't we just relax and enjoy ourselves?

Within days of arriving at our sugar-cane-harvesting work site, we presented them with an equally arrogant demand: This Venceremos Brigade was a waste of time for us, because, as they were aware, our organization was preparing to conduct armed struggle, and they should send us—the little leadership group, not all thirty Weatherpeople about whom we could have given a shit—home at once. You have a long struggle ahead, they replied, why not see what you can learn about socialism in these two months? We insisted. Of course, this was a decision that would have to be taken to higher-ups in Havana. They sent our demand to Havana. I still find it surprising that they took us that seriously.

We lived in dormitory tents scattered through a pretty grove of palm trees. Organized into work brigades of about thirty people, we would cut cane for a few hours in the morning, break for lunch and a rest in the heat of midday, and return to the fields in the afternoon. Meals were served cafeteria style in an enormous *bohio*—a thatch-roofed, open-sided pavilion; after lunch and dinner you lined up a second time for a thimbleful of intensely sweet and dark coffee, and if you were a guy, a cigar. In the evenings there were sometimes films in a simple amphitheater with palm logs as benches. One day Fidel Castro himself came to cut cane with us and make a speech. On weekends, and at the end of our six weeks of work, we were taken on trips around the island to see schools and clinics and other proud achievements of the Revolution. On one Sunday, we were turned loose in central Havana for an afternoon. People on the street offered us black market U.S. dollars for our jeans. Some gay boys we met in the park talked about how people like them could be sent to labor camps or jail. It is a measure of my credulousness at the time that this information about the desperation for Levi's and the bleak fate of homosexuals did not cause me to doubt the virtues of Castro's Cuba.

One day in early March, while we were awaiting a response to our demand to go home, during the peaceful free hour that followed the midday meal, when people napped or sat in the shade sharpening their machetes before going back to the cane fields, the bad news came. Someone with a shortwave radio had picked up a newscast from Miami. There had been an explosion, in New York, on 11th Street, and Teddy Gold had been killed. I grasped in an instant what had happened, although it would be a while before my intuition was confirmed and I learned any more details, including that Terry Robbins and Diana Oughton had also died. Cathy Wilkerson's father lived on 11th Street; I had once gone there with her. It was obvious to me. Our people had been using the place. Teddy had blown himself up.

The last time I saw Teddy was a few nights before I left Chicago for Cuba. We were crashing, along with a dozen of our comrades, at the apartment of one of our lawyers. We got there late. Everybody was asleep. We rummaged in the kitchen and found some ice cream. To not wake people up, we closed ourselves into the bathroom and sat facing each other in the empty tub, passing the carton back and forth, laughing and talking shit. Like, wouldn't it be outasight to set off a bomb at rush hour on an El train just as it crossed into the defiantly segregated white community of Cicero. The ice cream was Vala's, a superb but now-vanished Chicago brand. The flavor was caramel and cream, my favorite. Funny, what sticks with you.

• • •

Word came back from on high in Havana: Yes, we could go home. Now we weren't so sure that's what we wanted. We placed a call to our lawyers in Chicago. Without saying so explicitly, they conveyed that the organization had gone underground right after the town house explosion. So how would we find our people? The Cubans offered to fly us to Mexico City. But wouldn't incoming flights there from Cuba be monitored by the Americans? Sarah and Christine had both missed court dates. Were there warrants out for them now? Could we even cross the border back into the

U.S. without getting busted? Maybe we would be safer staying on the Brigade, going back on the ship to Canada with everyone else, and picking up that letter Mark had promised. Um, well, we told the authorities, this terrible thing has happened. They knew about it, and I don't think they were surprised at our sudden cold feet.

Soon they gave us more alarming news. A federal indictment had been issued for conspiracy to riot during the Days of Rage. I was named as an unindicted co-conspirator. We didn't know what that meant—there never were any real consequences for me—but in my grandiosity I liked to imagine the worst. The Cubans also passed on a cryptic and even more perplexing message that had come for us from the Weather Bureau: Don't return with the rest of the Brigade; stay in Cuba and wait for further instructions.

The prospect of additional limbo there was excruciating, so we hatched a new plan, and another demand. The Cubans should send us to Europe. From there we would figure out how to get home. They knew we weren't entirely inventing the risk of arrest, and they might even have empathized with our impatience. We were, however, a pain in the ass. I imagine they would have hosted us as long as necessary, but they agreed to dump us in Europe, no doubt with relief. The day before the Venceremos Brigade was to board a fleet of buses for the trip to the port in Havana and the ship for Canada, we were whisked away. Filmic intrigue: slipping unseen to meet behind the amphitheater, riding out of camp on a dusty track in an old DeSoto whose windows no longer went up, to a fading Fifties-modern hotel on the Malecón, which we were instructed not to leave. Underground, easy as that! And with those retro visuals, even more cinematic than imagined.

We waited in that hotel for a week, reading through a stack of recent American newsmagazines we'd been provided. Finally, space was found for us on a Cubana flight to Prague, and from there on a Czech Airlines flight to Frankfurt. The Cuban government declined to provide us with fake IDs, but they gave us some clothing and some cash. And a final message from our leaders at home—but too late, while we were already in a car on the way to the airport, on the very day we would have docked in St. John: It's okay, come back on the ship, a lawyer will be there to meet you. It felt like being slugged.

Paranoia and grandiosity: Since we had no choice but to use our own passports, we thought it was reasonable to expect that we would be nabbed at customs in the Frankfurt airport. I at least anticipated, and maybe even hoped for, a blaze of glory, though as a celebrity lit up for all to see by news photographers' flashbulbs, not a bloody one of bullets. But we were not in fact the subjects of an international police hunt. Even if we had been and even if, as we were convinced, the West Germans had been mere puppets of the U.S., the technology of the day wouldn't have been on their side. So there we were, free but an ocean away from home.

It was easy enough to melt into the international youth culture in Europe, to travel by hitchhiking, to find shelter and meals, even acquire hashish and casual sex. Our bigger challenge was to find fake ID so that we could return home under cover, on the self-aggrandizing theory that—never mind the failure of the Germans to bust us—we surely could not re-enter the U.S. under our own identities. Some of us tried to find ID in England, thinking that speaking the language would make the dead-baby-birth-certificate scam possible. I went to Stockholm, hoping that among the American deserters who had been given asylum by the Swedish government I might track down a source of false papers. Neither of these strategies panned out for us.

Discouraged by Stockholm, I was riding in a car back toward Frankfurt, where I had left some belongings at the apartment of an obliging student who had invited me to crash, when the driver translated the radio news bulletin that four antiwar demonstrators had been shot dead by National Guardsmen at Kent State University, in Ohio, and strikes were erupting at schools across the U.S. I had not expected being underground to place me in a state of useless suspension. But I was prevented by geography from relating to the protests at home, and by fear of discovery and arrest from joining the solidarity march I watched through a cafe window the next day in Frankfurt. Poor pitiful me, unable to contribute my voice or my body or my Molotov cocktail to the conflagration.

It was years before it occurred to me what else I and the rest of the Weather organization might have contributed to the massive popular reaction to Kent—and to the outrage over the U.S. invasion of Cambodia a few days earlier of which the Kent protest had been a part, and to the anger at the police shooting deaths of antiwar-demonstrating students at all-black Jackson State College in Mississippi that shortly followed it. That would have been the resources of the most influential and broadly connected radical organization of its time, which we had just finished destroying. But I couldn't have understood this then, because to me at the time all that mattered were armed action and secrecy.

Once my companions and I concluded that we weren't going to acquire false passports in Europe, we scrounged up money—with off-the-books restaurant gigs, money orders sent by relatives, outright thefts, and other hustles—and flew, one by one, to Canada, where it was easier to pretend we belonged. I actually pieced together a set of papers in Canada including a learner's permit and a library card—flimsy ID, but genuine. Then, also separately, we crossed back into the U.S. Again we weren't halted at the border, but in those days there was virtually no scrutiny on that border. We ended up in New York, where we stayed underground together, but on our own, out of touch with the Weather Underground, all the way until the last days of 1970. We tried to carry out the kind of work we thought we should be doing, making bombs and blowing things up. In our isolation, we replicated the madness of Weather politics. We never managed to succeed at bombing anything. We tried to make some explosive devices, but I am relieved now to say that we were incompetent at it.

I was the first to get to Canada, and was still on my own there when, browsing through the radical newspapers on a rack in a food co-op, I came upon a transcript of "the first communique from the Weatherman Underground," which had been released a few weeks earlier. It described the organization with exaggerated bravado. "There are several hundred members...and some of us face more years in jail than the fifty thousand deserters and draft dodgers now in Canada. Already many of them are coming back to join us in the underground." Both of these assertions, of the organization's considerable size and the stream of returning deserters, were untrue, but they were effective even on me, who should have known better. And where were my comrades? "In every tribe, commune, dormitory, farmhouse, barracks and town-house where kids are making love, smoking dope and loading guns—fugitives from Amerikan justice are free to go." There was a promise that they would carry out an armed action within two weeks. At first I felt deliriously happy reading this, as if I could reach out and touch them. Within minutes, the high deflated. They seemed to be enormous and growing, moving freely through the ephemeral networks of the counterculture and poised to strike. I was stranded and powerless and still not even back in the belly of the beast.

Then Sarah made it to Canada and contacted her cousin. There was no letter waiting for us. We couldn't know that Mark Rudd, to whom she had given the address, had been kicked from leadership. He had probably forgotten that he ever had that matchbook in his coat pocket. We were still resentful at having been sent to Cuba in the first place. It had led on to this elaborate waste of time in Europe and Canada—we ignored the facts that Europe and Canada had been our own scheme, and that the Weather leadership had kept in contact with us, if confusingly, while we were in Cuba. We leapt to the entirely delusional conclusion that we had been deliberately cast adrift.

Later, after this long strange detour had ended and we were back in touch with the organization, we learned that they had been worried and looking for us. There were people with whom they were in touch whom they thought we might contact, who knew to loop us back in immediately. If we had been rational, we might have thought of that, and realized who those intermediaries would be. It was our paranoid fantasy that we had been rejected, and it was also our paranoid fantasy that the cops were so magically pervasive and all-knowing that we dared not contact anyone who had the slightest association with Weatherman, or even SDS.

In fact, once we got to New York one or another of us did occasionally cross paths with people we knew, some of whom we later learned were among those who would have reconnected us. But we always ran the other way in panic, as if each of them was certainly shadowed every moment by an FBI agent who would recognize and bust us on the spot. This twisted mentality was a logical outcome of our experience in the Weather Machine, with its apocalyptic view of the outside world and its self-esteem-eroding internal culture, cooked down to sludge by our isolated and overheated imaginations. It was not a necessary outcome of having been in Weatherman, but we could not have lived it had it not been a possible one.

• • •

After Stockholm and Frankfurt, I had hitched to Paris. In school I studied French, and could speak it a little. I was in Paris for a few days at age eleven, when my family was traveling home from Taipei, but I certainly didn't know the city. Except in imagination. And it was a dream Paris that drew me: the romance of glamorous boulevards and ancient narrow streets; the romance of clandestinity, based on stories of the World War II French Resistance; the romance of the student-led rebellion in '68; the romance of romance, from movies and books, such as *Giovanni's Room*.

There was something I wanted to do that I sensed could be done in Paris: I would try earning money through prostitution.

No big deal, y'know—there were those Weatherwomen who gave hand jobs to truckers, and all that. At first I pictured myself hanging out in the bars of classy hotels and playing gigolo to rich divorcees. But I never actually gave that a try. My real intention was to pick up men. I did need the money. I needed to find a bed every night, too. But I also needed to explore my sexuality. I was alone and unknown, which made me oddly unafraid; no one whom I knew could see me doing this. I was audacious—was I not a Weatherman? And I had just been doing physical work in the tropical sun for two months. I was tanned, there were natural highlights in my hair, I was more fit than I'd ever been. Several factors seemed to make this a viable plan. Most important among them, I was eager to do it.

How is it possible that I already knew the secret language of cruising? Is it encoded in gene Xq28 along with the tendency to homosexuality itself? I had used it already in Frankfurt, and it got me two nights in a luxury hotel with a very nice English fashion designer, room-service breakfast and discreet gift of cash included. I liked that, the money and the luxury, and the pleasurable intimacy. So I hustled men in Paris, and after that in Montreal and then in New York. Some people who do sex work are forced into it, or can see no alternative, but I chose it and undertook it from a position of strength. My class background was an asset; I was a decent conversationalist, a presentable dinner companion. I never found myself threatened, never picked up a sexually transmitted disease or crab lice as I had during the Weather Machine. I made decent money hustling. I was lucky, no doubt, perhaps even gifted at this.

Not every encounter was entirely pleasant, but most were interesting to me, and educational. These were the early days of the famously promiscuous gay Seventies, and I never found much difference between the hookups I had for fun in those years and the ones I was paid for. The sex itself may or may not have been memorable, in either context, but both were likely to lead to that moment of confiding and revelation, to the shared fragment of the other guy's story. It's what my friend the queer writer Andrew Ramer has called "the weaving of the tribe." Promiscuity erupted among gay men in the Seventies because suddenly we believed we could have what had been denied. Sex had been denied, but our stories had been, too. We were starved for touch with each other, of both kinds.

I'm glad I had those experiences, but I am not without a certain wistfulness about them. I took advantage of being underground to explore my sexuality, but I was doing it in secret. That freed me by removing the possibility of judgment by anyone whose judgment mattered to me. But I kept myself secret from the men I met, too. As much as I took from these encounters, and gave physically, I was not fully present. I craved their true stories, but I fabricated my own, or dissembled. These men—some of them— showed the possibility of a proud *out* life, but I didn't allow myself to step toward it. I was stuck with that static self-image as a revolutionary, and couldn't reframe that in a way that let me be whole. I was twenty-two then; you will recall that I did not come out for another twenty years.

Of the dozens or scores of men I went with during 1970, three lingered in memory. I still recalled their names, long after I'd forgotten all the others', still felt the impressions they had made. Only later did I come to learn that each was an individual of bravery and creativity, an important person in the world. If I had fully engaged with any one of them I might have saved myself years of hiding. I don't think I would necessarily have been lovers or even lifelong friends with any one of them. But as a role model or a mentor, someone I would let in, any one of them could have changed my life. My life is fine now. I'm deeply glad to have arrived where I am, married to Peter, with a gratifying career, living in an extremely beautiful and, as the Chinese curse has it, interesting place. Still, it is striking to me that by chance I should have crossed paths with these three particular men, and not seen who they were. But we already know that I wasn't seeing clearly.

In Paris, I was at the bar in a gay club so grown-up and understated that it barely had a sign, and certainly had no pounding music, when Gerald Messadié took the stool next to mine. I went home with him, in his Jaguar, to his elegant apartment off the Champs-Élysées. I'm amazed now to recall that within a few minutes of meeting, I asked him to give me plane fare to Canada. He agreed, but only if I would spend a week with him first. He also insisted on buying the ticket, not handing me cash. I of course had given him a phony name, so now I'd have to tell my real one, but I didn't hesitate. He put me in a hotel, and we met every evening. He wanted me to stay and live with him. He would buy me a car, take me to Biarritz for the summer. I knew he was rich, and erudite, and cosmopolitan, an editor of something. I didn't bother to find out more; I was just using him, and I was leaving. For years after that, when I felt stuck or bereft or a failure, I thought of going to him if he would have me. But I never called. Thirty years after we met in 1970, Gerald saw an article of mine in an airline magazine and tracked me down. I have visited him since then, the few times I've returned to Paris since 2000, and know more about him now. He is an editor, essayist, historian, novelist—and iconoclast. He has published about fifty books. When I first saw him again he was dealing with blowback for his most recent one, a history of antisemitism in France that was making a lot of people squirm. Gerald is imperious and cranky now, and maybe he always was. Maybe he only has a place in my heart because he pursued me so flatteringly. But he took me seriously, saw something in me, even when he knew I was keeping secrets.

I met Jean Basile Bezroudnoff in a park in Montreal. I wasn't after money that night; I thought we looked enough alike that I might get by using his ID, which I intended to steal. Over dinner I learned that he reviewed pop music for a newspaper, and was interested in radical politics; Quebecois separatism was in the air, and we discussed it. Later we drove to his place, in his Pontiac convertible with the top down. We smoked some pot, and he played the newest Grateful Dead album, prodding me for my reactions and taking notes. When I thought he was asleep, I took his wallet into the bathroom but there wasn't anything in it with a description or a photo, so I just put it back. In the morning, he surprised me by asking why I had taken it but not taken anything from it. I said I'd been planning to steal money but decided I liked him too much. I saw Jean a few more times, but I didn't bother getting to know him; I was just using him, and I was leaving. Not long ago, I found his traces online. He didn't just review music for *Le Devoir*—signing his pieces "Penelope"—but for years had been editor of its Arts and Letters section. During the Sixties—before Stonewall—he had written a trilogy of novels that included gay characters and themes, among the first in Quebecois literature that did. Shortly after I knew him, he co-founded a radical monthly, *Mainmise*; it means "stranglehold." Jean became a publisher, and continued to write novels, essays, and plays on queer themes and on drug culture, the tarot, and tantric sex. He died in 1992, at sixty.

A man I met on the street in New York and went home with just for fun suggested that his friend Jack Deveau could introduce me to a madam—a guy who kept a rolodex of affluent johns and a stable of boys to set them up with. I called Jack. Feeling, I suppose, that he should determine how well I'd do before recommending me to the madam, he invited me to dinner. His place was a cool penthouse with a fabulous view. I sipped wine while he cooked. He was wry and charming. It was a rare pleasure to have a normal meal in someone's home. We got high; I stayed the night with him and his partner, Robert. I saw Jack a few more times, but I didn't bother to find out much more about him than that he was a filmmaker; I was just using him, and I was leaving. Now I understand that he was perhaps the most important producer and director of gay porn in that period, because along with beefcake and fucking his films had narrative and story arcs, developed characters and plausible dialogue, and visual experimentation. Jack died in 1982, at forty-seven. His work is still screened at queer film festivals and considered in gender studies programs. While he was cooking me dinner that first night, he worked himself up about President Nixon, the right wing, and political repression. "It's coming down," he insisted. "They're going to be looking for scapegoats, and just watch, they're going to come after gay people. Who else is left? They've just about killed all the Panthers, and *nobody even knows where the Weathermen are.*"

• • •

Nobody. Including me.

Our tiny grouplet had rejected the Weather Underground on the grounds that it had rejected us. But in my moments of transition between the bleak, minuscule hothouse of our secret cell and the seductively entertaining world of hustling, I would feel desolated. I longed for my friends in Weatherman. One night at a disco I saw a guy who looked startlingly like Mike Spiegel, except that he was blond. But we all had dyed hair then—mine was black. Maybe he *is* Mike, I thought. I asked him to dance, and then went home with him, desperate to draw out what I of course knew was an unsupportable fantasy. Sometimes I pretended that when I rounded the next corner I would run into Karin. Sometimes I would will a woman in the subway car to turn in my direction and be Phoebe. More than once, alone, at night, walking streets I had walked with them, with Jeff, I wept.

We couldn't ignore forever the futility of our plan to conduct armed action on our own. Our idea of armed action was bombing, perhaps because bombs are spectacular, or perhaps because that's what the Weather Underground was doing every now and then. Despite resenting the organization we were still in thrall to it. But we lacked both the technical skills and practical resources to make bombs. It never occurred to us to try something in the mode of terrorist attack more common today, such as walking into a target location and shooting the place up, even though acquiring guns would have been quite easy. Despite our slogans about revolutionary suicide, we must have known that a shootout was far more likely to mean real suicide, whereas a bomb could be placed hours before it detonated, allowing plenty of time to disappear. Unless the bomb blew up as you were assembling it.

After a few months in New York, we began to acknowledge our paralyzing isolation. For a while we tried various ways of finding sympathetic people we might "organize" into some kind of support network. We would hang out near high schools in the afternoons and try to find kids with whom we could get into political raps, à la the Weather collectives of the previous summer. The meetings of consciousness-raising groups were sometimes advertised in *The Village Voice*. I went to one for gay men and recognized in panic, after I'd already taken off my coat and sat down, that the guy leading it was Jim Fouratt, a longtime activist who had attended events where I'd been and might have recognized me if he'd looked past my fake glasses and dyed hair.

Jim was probably not one of those people the Weather Bureau had told to keep an eye out for us. But he probably was someone who would have been supportive, if I had identified myself. In the wider movement, at the time, there was enormous pride in the Weather Underground for being bold and for eluding capture, and plenty of people who disapproved of us were still willing to help us. But all I felt, recognizing Jim, was the danger of being discovered. Of course, the point of a consciousness-raising group is precisely discovery—revelation, true stories, commonality. My idea that while wearing the disguise—the armor—of secrecy, I might develop any authentic bonds in a consciousness-raising group was ludicrous. I never went back.

The time came when we couldn't stand it anymore. Any one of us might have done something to bust the situation open. As it happened, Christine ran across someone she knew, from one of the Weather collectives, and instead of fleeing as was our usual reaction she said hello. That person was still in the organization and knew we were being looked for. Just like that, thanks to a chance encounter on the subway and a chink we had allowed to open in our armor, we were able to reconnect.

First they requested a meeting with me alone, at the Brooklyn Public Library. I stood at the top of the steps, not knowing who I was waiting for. For hustling, I had cultivated a pulled-together presentation: good haircut, fashionable topcoat, Italian loafers with thin soles in place of the shitkicking motorcycle boots of the Machine days. Bill Ayers came up the steps dressed in the counterculture regalia of shaggy hair, jeans, moccasins, and beads, and didn't recognize me at first. We spent an hour in a diner while I told him our tale.

We saw Bill, Jeff, and Bernardine several times in the following days. We got high together. I took a ride on the Staten Island Ferry with the guys. There was a trip to the movies to see the revival of *Fantasia*, of all things. Bill gave me a gift, the piercing of my ear, and a silver stud that I wore as an emblem of welcome back. Indeed, a pierced ear, for men, was now a common element in the uniform of the Weather Underground, which was the camouflage of hippie style. That was of a piece with where the organization had hidden itself, in the amorphous, permeable counterculture. Nobody wore shitkickers anymore. And the kind of gambol and frolic we'd just experienced with Jeff, Bill, and Bernardine seemed to have become the order of the day. The look and the ostensibly idle, pleasure-seeking affect of youth culture were protective coloration like that which makes certain insects disappear against a backdrop of leaves. In fact, so as not to attract the attention of, say, other diners in a restaurant who might accidentally overhear—or be deliberately eavesdropping—the jargon now for the underground was "the forest," while the rest of the world, everything not underground, was "the ocean." The forest was a place to hide. The ocean, so vast and blurry, could be swum with invisibility.

Very quickly, their message to us was clear: What you're doing is unnecessary and, um, silly. Go settle your legal problems and swim in the ocean. That's what they told us as a group. To me, aside, they gave another message: We will stay in touch. Suddenly set free, I decided to head for San Francisco, where my three siblings had all moved during the preceding year. Jeff would be there as well by the time I arrived, and we arranged a way to be in touch. "Decide how you're going to look," he advised. "Pick one look and keep it. If you're going to grow a beard, don't shave it. Disguises aren't that easy and you want to keep your options open." Perhaps, I heard him saying—or, hoped he was saying—I would be rejoining them, underground. I still believed that being part of a clandestine, militaristic organization was the most glorious way to live. Or more accurately, I thought of it as the most romantic way to live. That the endlessly escalating confrontations of the Machine had been replaced with this psychedelic love-in on the barricades made it more romantic still. Once I had pictured anxious secret meetings in cold basements lit by bare bulbs hanging on cords. Now I imagined plans being sagely considered, as the pipe was passed, around a campfire under the stars.

The first person I contacted to announce my reappearance in the visible world was Marge Piercy, my friend and mentor from the New York SDS staff. She was as likely as anybody to have a tapped phone line, so with a call to her I considered that I had revealed myself to the police, and surfaced. That evening found me at her table, cosseted by warmth and concern that transcended her wariness of the path I—we—had taken. "Right after that," Marge reminded me years later, "I gave a big New Year's Eve party. It was your first 'public appearance.' I was worried about you, because you seemed nervous. But then you were flirting with everybody and seemed to be on top of the world." I did feel elated, possibly more than I ever had. The hellfire hurricane of the Machine was over. My bizarrely isolated and dualistic life since Cuba was over. My friends still loved me. They had told me that I had no legal problems, so I was free that way, too.

I gave away my classy clothes. I left New York to hitchhike across the country. Along the way I dropped acid with strangers. I watched the sun rise from a mesa in New Mexico. I got a ride with a band of freaks in an old school bus, among whom were two young dykes on a mission to spread the amazing news that cancer could be cured by chaparral tea. I loved them! I loved that they were an out lesbian couple! I believed them! Chaparral could cure cancer, and it was growing wild right there all over the hillsides!

I was California Dreaming. On a radiant warm day I passed through L.A., and the next guy who gave me a ride handed me yet another tab of acid. I watched the golden surfers at Malibu, and stared into the sunset from the back of a Harley zooming up the Pacific Coast Highway. My last ride into San Francisco was with a different bunch of freaks, in a VW microbus that was creeping its way up a steep road in the middle of the night, heading inland toward the city. Rounding a curve, we saw a red light flashing up through the trees from somewhere far below: the blinker of a car that had plunged off into the canyon. This must be a sign, but of what? Everything was mystical, violet-tinged, drenched in significance.

• • •

It's starting to seem as if everybody of a certain age whom I tell about this book trots out a claim to personal connection with Weatherman. They were at the Days of Rage; or have a cousin or college roommate who was a collective member, or was underground; or they once sheltered somebody who was on the run, or lent a car. It's the same phenomenon as everybody who was under thirty and on the East Coast in 1969 claiming to have been at Woodstock, or half the gay men who were alive that same year saying they fought in the Stonewall riot. That's okay. I understand the impulse to identify with a history that was important and still is. I also know that recollections blur, and false memories can be confabulated from fragments of truth glued together with wishful thinking. Besides, I'm not in a position to verify other people's experiences of Weatherman, aside from those I personally witnessed, and I don't even recollect all of those clearly.

A friend of Peter's and mine here in the Hudson Valley, John Mahoney, was only a little boy during the years I am describing. He makes no claim to personal connection, but still had a unique link to offer. John is a designer, and has been working on collateral products for art museums. One of his clients now is the Cleveland Museum of Art. He was noodling around for fresh ideas and found this: An original casting of *The Thinker*, made under August Rodin's direct supervision, was donated to the museum in 1917 and placed outside on a plinth, where it acquired a rich bronze-green patina. It was bombed in March of 1970. The Cleveland police immediately attributed this act to a Weatherman cell it claimed was operating in the city. The sculpture remained more or less intact but lost its feet and lower legs, and was a bit twisted and banged up. (Lost feet, banged up: That's what happened to people standing too close to the backpack bomb at the Boston Marathon a couple of years ago, too.) Without being repaired, *The Thinker* was put back in place.

John Mahoney has an artist's sense of irony and layered meaning. He proposed using the image of the damaged sculpture on mugs and tote bags or whatever. The idea didn't fly, despite the fact that the museum director at the time had said, "Is it not even a more significant work, damaged as it is? No one can pass the shattered green man without asking himself what it tells us about the violent climate of the U.S.A. in the year 1970." My knowledge of Weather actions is not encyclopedic, but I had never heard of this incident before—and it had never been claimed by the organization. Besides, that attribution just didn't feel quite right. Mike had not heard of it, either, and agrees that the cops must have been wrong. "That was too rarefied and intellectual. Is dadaist the word? We were never that subtle."

After the town house explosion that killed Teddy, Terry, and Diana and precipitated the quick transition into hiding by the Weathermen, the organization did some soul searching. It disavowed the idea of attacking people. But it continued to embrace the tactic of bombing. Between the town house accident in March 1970, and the time I arrived in California in January 1971, at least five more bombings were claimed by the Weather Underground, of targets including various courthouses and the headquarters of the New York Police Department. In the same period there were at least another fifteen bombings in the U.S. that logically would have been the work of leftists but were not claimed by the Weather Underground—although one does wonder about several unclaimed ones that have a distinct Weather vibe, like a repeat bombing of that statue of the policeman in Chicago's Haymarket Square. (I don't include *The Thinker* in that count because my take on the Cleveland attack is that it was the work of artists who perhaps despised the sculpture as a cliché, made kitsch by its appropriation for the TV show *The Many Loves of Dobie Gillis* and countless cheap replicas sold in tourist traps the world over. They may not have considered themselves political or ideological at all. Or maybe they were pissed off that the museum wouldn't show their own work. Or maybe they were just plain crazy.)

But you get the picture: Terrorist acts like bombings and hijackings were frequent in the Sixties, a toxic bloom that has never ceased spreading. The Weather Underground was blowing things up, and so were a lot of other people. The issue of *The Atlantic* that just arrived in my mailbox this week astonished me with the mention that "from January 1969 to April 1970, more than 8,200 bomb threats, attempted bombings, and actual bombings were attributed to student protests." Of course, the U.S. already had a long history of armed terrorist acts—bombings, shootouts, assassinations, lynchings—perpetrated by anarchists, communists, separatists and paramilitaries of various stripes, the Ku Klux Klan and other racists. The Weather Underground claimed that it never injured anyone else after the town house, which may be true. But it is reasonable to suppose that its incendiary rhetoric and its actions led others to attempt bombings, too. At that moment in history, Weatherman had a mighty big megaphone. It claimed leadership of the radical movement. Many people were listening. Why should we discount the possibility that some people would have felt encouraged by it?

In August 1970, a bombing of the Army Mathematics Research Center at the University of Wisconsin killed a physics post-doc who was there pulling an all-nighter. The bombers were four guys like us, radical students who hated the war in Vietnam and, like us, had given up on the idea that peaceful protest would have any effect. They may or may not have ever been involved with SDS but surely were aware of, and very possibly inspired by, Weatherman.

A particularly spectacular attack was a dynamite-fueled, nail-filled anti-personnel bomb set off at lunchtime in the historic Fraunces Tavern, in Manhattan's financial district in 1975, which killed four and injured forty-three. It was the work of a Marxist-Leninist Puerto Rican separatist group. The Weather Underground was vociferously supportive of the armed actions of the Puerto Rican separatist movement.

Especially over recent years bombers and assault-rifle attackers have more commonly been anti-abortionists, white nationalists, actors from both sides of the Israeli-Palestinian conflict, homophobes, and of course now Islamic jihadis. It's also plainly the case that despite what rhetoric they may recite, some of the perpetrators may not be all that ideological. Some may be pissed off about some personal slight, or maybe just plain crazy. Or have some braiding of these traits that can't be unraveled.

But every action is liable to elicit a not-necessarily-equal reaction. Just three days ago, on October 15, 2016, a Republican campaign office in North Carolina was firebombed, presumably by someone who might prefer a Democrat as president. What scares me about this crazily polarizing election we're living through as I write is its invigoration and provocation of people who, just like the guys who killed the young physicist in Wisconsin in 1970, believe that the government no longer hears them. Now, thanks to whoever bombed the campaign office, there may well be members of that cohort who feel they must hit back, and that this attack has given them permission to do so.

After 1970, the Weather Underground took credit for another dozen or more bombings. The targets included the U.S. Capitol, the Pentagon, various other government buildings, and offices of several international—read: imperialist—corporations like Gulf Oil and Anaconda Copper. Warnings were issued in advance, to help ensure that the buildings would be cleared. The devices were modest in power, typically slipped into air vents in restrooms—these were still the years when anybody who looked blandly anonymous could walk unimpeded into such places without the slightest security check.

There are former Weatherpeople who insist that these careful actions, sanitized of injury to human beings, were merely symbolic and not terroristic. Benign as leaflets, they imply; like guerrilla theater. When they say this, you can almost smell the patchouli oil and hear the rattling love beads that costumed the Weather Underground's gentle-warrior persona. But this assumes the narrowest definition of terrorism as only what injures or kills people. It elides the psychological and cultural ramifications of violent actions.

Weatherman was bent on terrorism up until the town house explosion. What about later, after the accidental suicide by dynamite there of our three comrades had prompted the shift to careful bombings that hurt no one? At times I have thought, and written, that we never stopped being terrorists. Now I think this is not the most important question. Answer it however you like. We didn't invent terrorism, but we did contribute to its momentum. If that contribution was restrained, even negligible, later, it had been ardent and reckless earlier, and there is no retrieving energy already released.

You may be aggravated or bemused by my considering that the Weather Underground was terrorist. Many people idealize the organization, still, as simply a group of charismatic, romantic outlaws. And for my generation, terrorism crept into consciousness slowly and incrementally, so it's hard to connect those little symbolic Weather bombings of yesteryear, doing minor damage in the bathrooms of meaningful targets, with the wanton slaughter we nowadays see so often. Meanwhile, younger people have grown up with an awareness of terrorism on a large scale and as a constant possibility—and with the awareness that they themselves might well be its intended victims. (I'm not referring here to the terrorism against people of color in the U.S., which has always been going on. Most white people have been oblivious to that, and it is still not widely named or understood as terrorism, though perhaps that's changed a bit recently.) The intellectual frameworks and stated goals that we had in Weatherman are hugely different from those of your garden variety twenty-first-century terrorist. But the emotional impulses behind our actions and theirs might not be so dissimilar. Today's terrorism is typically more relentless and spectacular and, well, terrifying, than what the Weather Underground and kindred New Left grouplets ever did, though it's not so different from what some of us wanted to do at certain moments, and would have done if we'd been able. If my town house comrades had been successful, the destruction at the dance they intended to blow up in 1970 would have looked an awful lot like what happened just recently in Orlando, at Pulse.

From its founding to its demise, Weatherman existed in a matrix of violence, and contributed to the escalation of violence and the desensitization to violence that have extended through the world ever since. The Weather Underground helped create this reality we inhabit now in which blowing things up and shooting places up are considered by some people to be legitimate ways of advancing a cause. When I say the Weather Underground here I mean me, too, although I was never personally involved in any of the organization's bombing actions, not because I objected or would have refused, but just because I was never asked. Had I been, I would have happily sat around that campfire under the whispering pines, passing that joint and helping make those plans.

· · ·

Or would I have?

I am encountering a little grammatical problem here, as you may have noticed, to do with whether to consistently use the first person or the third person. For example: "The Weather Underground claimed that it never injured anyone else..." I was a member of the Weather Underground, so wouldn't it be more accurate, and honest, for me to say "We never injured..."?

On one hand, unlike the Machine days in 1969 when I was often the senior person present at the National Office and by default, or because I was instructed to, answered queries from the press, it was not I who was doing the claiming now. And since all I knew about those bombings was whatever was put forth publicly by the leadership, I wouldn't have known the facts about, for example, what we might now call collateral damage. It has been alleged and I believe it is possible, for example, that some actions were never claimed by the organization because they had not gone according to plan. That almost certainly does not include, I hasten to add, the lack of claim for the attack on *The Thinker*, which as Mike suggested was too much a nuanced gesture of cultural criticism to ever have been our handiwork—if cultural criticism it was, and not just the lark of some nutcase who got a thrill when things go boom and decided to make one do so himself.

But on the other hand, consider something else I wrote above: "The Weather Underground was vociferously supportive of the armed actions of the Puerto Rican separatist movement."

Why doesn't it come naturally for me to say, "We were vociferously supportive," since I willingly added my voice to that chorus? I can no longer access a memory of this, but it is possible and even likely that I cheered the 1975 bombing of Fraunces Tavern and its toll of four dead. Wall Street trash, I might have dismissed the victims as being, just crumpled paper tossed along the gutter by the blast wave. I'm quite sure I never learned any of those victims' names, nor a single detail of their actual human lives. If they weren't human to me, and I applauded the Puerto Rican militants' anti-personnel attack, what would have stopped me from planting a perfectly harmless little bomb in an office building men's room?

I was asked to do a lot of things by the Weather Underground leadership over the years and, toward the end, asked to do many things I didn't even believe at the time were right, but I did them anyway. I let my friends talk me into doing them. Those acts mainly amounted to lying to people, rather than potentially injuring them. When I finally quit it was not just because I realized that the vision was unconnected to reality. Even then, as ever, I was acting more from emotion than ideology. Mostly I was angry at having been manipulated, and humiliated for allowing myself to be manipulated, and mortified at then manipulating others in turn. But no one ever asked me to carry out a bombing. Grown-up me wants to think that even if they had, as late in the process, say, as the moment when dressed in the bland costume of an office worker I had been handed the attaché case containing the ticking device, I would have hesitated, considered the implications, and declined to go through with it. But I was still a child during those years, who needed to tag along after the big boys, take their dare, win their approval. Yes, almost certainly, I would have done it.

• • •

In the Bay Area, I moved freely in activist circles, attending occasional meetings and demonstrations. But I was also in frequent contact with people who were underground, through calls between pay phones. I often met them in person. The content of these encounters was almost entirely social. The only tangible work I did was to pass along messages to supporters and hit them up for money. Sometimes I visited the home of Bill, Jeff, and Bernardine, who were the leaders of the Weather Underground's Bay Area operation. That was a spacious, though barely furnished, modern house in an affluent suburb. They had cars and money and marijuana. We would get high and cook dinner, or go walking in the hills. They must have appeared to their neighbors as hippie aristocracy, rock musicians between tours perhaps—since they obviously didn't have jobs. Sometimes I would meet with one of my other friends who was a fugitive; those who weren't in leadership lived grouped in apartments and typically got around on public transportation; those visits weren't so fun. The difference in living conditions reflected an internal class system that persisted throughout the underground years—another face of the organization's corruption.

While I was underground in New York, Timothy Leary, the former Harvard professor who became a promoter of LSD and had been jailed on drug charges, was freed by the Weather Underground. In my little grouplet we scorned this action; we could name numerous imprisoned revolutionaries more important to liberate, most of whom had brown skin and harsher sentences. The Weather Underground's spin was that they had freed Leary because he was a counterculture hero and so this was a victory for rebellious kids everywhere. A former member later pointed out to me that Leary was freed because it was possible—he was in a low-security prison—and because his drug world friends paid the organization for the service. Leary soon arrived to seek asylum in Algeria in the company of a "Miss Dohrn," not Bernardine but her sister Jennifer. Jennifer to my knowledge had been nowhere near SDS or the Weather Machine. She'd been in some obscure Marxist-Leninist cadre in L.A. working a factory job. Now she had traded doctrinaire proletarian drudgery for the Weather Underground's more colorful and breezy lifestyle and put herself forward as the organization's most public supporter.

I met Jennifer at a party in Berkeley, soon after I got to the Bay Area. We quickly began to think of ourselves as a couple and as "running partners," a team. Showing up in Algiers with Timothy Leary, she had made herself instantly notorious—she not only shared Bernardine's last name, but also her photogenic looks, and she was willing to act as stand-in. I wasn't known in the media but I was known in the movement. Now and then Jennifer would be invited to speak, or give an interview. I was along as aide de camp and companion. It looks mighty superficial now, the haze of incense and pot smoke, our stoned wonder at everything from rainbows to tricks for scamming the welfare department out of food stamps, the occasional appearance at a radical event, the mellow drives to the beach in borrowed cars, the mooching off supporters. Speaking of corruption. We weren't doing any organizing or grounded work, just being political personalities—famous for being famous in the radical movement, as it might be described today.

I loved the intimacy I had with Jennifer, the assumption of mutual protection as a priority; it was something I hadn't ever experienced. And I basked in the special way I was treated by the underground leaders. I was special because I had been Jeff's longtime friend, and then close with Bill, and was now taking care of Bernardine's sister about whose vulnerability they all worried. And special because I had been lost, and after my weird detour maybe special because they weren't sure just how durable my sanity might be. Actually, Jennifer and I were more running partners than we ever were a couple, although we told the world we were a couple, because I wasn't able to be much of a lover to her, which surely was hard for her. And after a few months she put an end to the fiction, and we stopped living together, although we remained close friends, until the organization broke apart.

One of the genuine achievements of the Weather Underground, and one source of its persistent romance, was keeping so many people successfully hidden for years, many of them fugitives, without being discovered. But in the Bay Area in that spring of 1971 there was a series of close calls that almost busted the organization. It became known among us as "the encirclement." My frequent shuttling between ocean and forest surely contributed to the near-disaster. There are, in my FBI file, accurate descriptions of me driving to make and receive phone calls. There was a day when I was walking down a street in San Francisco, actually on my way to a rendezvous with a fugitive, when a police car suddenly drove up onto the sidewalk, pinning me against a fence. The cops found the false ID I was carrying, and booked me on "possession of stolen property." A few days later the charges were dropped without another word. They kept the ID, of course, authentic documents in an assumed name that I had spent months piecing together while I was underground. That name shows up in subsequent FBI memos as an alias I might be expected to use— although I never understood why they thought I would use it, now that they had it.

There were multiple breaches. Maybe that house in the suburbs had been a risky choice, and the neighbors suspected its occupants of being dope dealers, or radical fugitives, and made a call? One morning I arrived there in a borrowed car. Parked across the road was a sedan with two suits in it. "What do you think that's about?" I asked Bill when he opened the door. He took one look and called down the hall in alarm. Jeff and Bernardine started furiously packing, while Bill and I followed the car into town where it parked in the courthouse lot. Minutes after we got back, my friends abandoned their house.

The exposures began to cascade. Fugitives were identified and followed, their apartments were invaded minutes after they had escaped out rear windows, cars and precious false ID had to be left behind. Barely in time, the pattern was recognized. The Bay Area Weather Underground pulled way back, suspending contact with supporters. I got the message that Jennifer and I should go someplace else. On April Fool's Day 1971, we boarded a plane for Chicago.

• • •

For the next few months, Jennifer and I replicated what we had been doing in the Bay Area, on a wider geographic scale: traveling around, often together but sometimes not, allowing people to think that we were representatives of the underground, making press appearances and going on demonstrations, and continuing to sponge off supporters—chief among them the Chicago collective of lawyers who had defended the Weather Machine. By the end of the summer, she had decided to extricate herself from our illusory coupledom and live in New York.

I was mostly hanging around in Chicago, without a focus. Only Susan Jordan, one of those lawyers, had the nerve to challenge me. Older than I, she had first been a journalist, then an inner-city teacher, had gone South to register black voters, and then became a defense attorney. She had figured out that there were productive things she could do in life and then organized her life to do them, and didn't see why I shouldn't, too. Also she was pissed off at me because I had borrowed her brand-new lemon-yellow VW bug for a trip out of town, lost the key, and then broken the window and smashed the steering wheel lock in order to hotwire the car. And had not paid for the repair. Susan was fierce. It wasn't pleasant to be challenged for my bad behavior, but I'm still glad she did it.

I stayed in Chicago, and I figured out that I am a writer. At first I tried to write a novel, supporting myself with a series of part-time jobs. For a few months, I taught in an ephemeral "free school," where my class consisted of three six-year-old boys, and my complete lack of qualification was not considered an obstacle. Then I drove a cab, until I had an accident and was fired. Then I fell in with a group of actual journalists who were starting what is now called an alt weekly. *The Chicago Express* was launched at exactly the moment, with a nearly identical concept, as *The Chicago Reader.* The *Reader* is still around, while the *Express* failed after a couple of years. But it was a job, and gave me practice as a feature writer and knowledge of how a serious publication is produced, worthwhile preparation for the career in magazines I eventually built and still enjoy.

I found a cheap apartment in a lively neighborhood—later it became Boystown, though in the early Seventies the population was mainly a congenial mix of counterculture types and recently arrived Puerto Rican immigrants. A loose social scene evolved among some of the residents of my apartment house; everybody's kitchen door opened onto a back porch that ran the length of the building. We were in and out of each other's places often, sharing communal dinners, partying together. I even had that emblem of normalcy, a checking account, for the first time in years. It was almost a life. Except that I was never fully engaged, because I also had a secret life.

My contact with the underground had been re-established. For the next two years, while I lived in Chicago, where the Weather organization didn't have an underground presence, I made regular phone calls and paid occasional visits to my fugitive friends. I was under frequent police surveillance, so I organized clandestine relationships with several people who had political sympathy or personal loyalties but no public history with the organization. I would call on them to donate money or shelter someone who was passing through, or to help me maintain my own ability to function securely. Some received mail for me, envelopes sealed within envelopes. In somebody's guest-room closet, I kept a suitcase containing false ID, different clothes, a pair of fake glasses. Whenever I was on my way into the forest for a visit I would stop there to trade my own for these, after first having taken a couple of buses and altered direction until I knew I was not followed. Then I would go on to my meeting, adding additional diversions like going by train to Milwaukee and flying from there to meet people in New York, instead of using O'Hare.

It was always Jeff on the phone, and when I visited underground, which I did a couple of times a year, I would see him and other old friends. Which left me elated—and conflicted. Life underground was hard for them, their movements constrained, social lives restricted, money tight. I felt guilty for having my almost normal life. I also desperately wanted to be underground with them myself. Early on, I asked for that, and was denied. I had no need to be in hiding and they didn't need the burden of supporting another person underground; besides, they did need the support I could provide from where I was. But my intense emotional involvement with this remote and hidden thing from which I was isolated by geography kept me lonely, and depressed. I began to worry that my personality was being deformed, since I wouldn't allow myself to be fully present emotionally in my visible life, while I couldn't be present physically with the people in my secret life. Duality and tension must be inevitable for anybody doing illegal work and keeping big secrets. But does every clandestine operative suffer from a love jones for his organization?

By the spring of 1973, I had decided that I couldn't keep it up. Either I was going to be brought closer, or I was going to wish my friends luck and see them again after the revolution. I made another visit underground, which I spent almost entirely with Mike. He convinced me that my going underground couldn't be justified, and helped me picture other scenarios. Why didn't I focus as a writer on some political arena, he suggested, like Wilfred Burchett, whose war dispatches from Indochina we had followed for years, or Basil Davidson, who wrote vividly about anti-colonial movements in Africa? Mike said, "Find some struggle you want to work with. Study it. Go there. Make a life for yourself." Suppose I did, and spent years in Latin America or Africa? It really could mean an indefinite separation from the Weather Underground. Could I stand it?

Faster than we could have imagined I found myself deeply involved as a writer in a stirring movement. It wasn't so far away, and it did not become my life's work, and also didn't force me to lose touch with the organization for any great length of time. By the time I got back to Chicago after that visit with Mike, Wounded Knee was in the news. Members of the traditional Oglala Sioux community on the Pine Ridge Indian Reservation in South Dakota had taken a stand—with guns, and with people who knew how to use them, like Vietnam vets. They had occupied the village of Wounded Knee where, in 1890, three hundred unarmed Sioux had been massacred by U.S. soldiers. The protesters were demanding an end to the corrupt and thuggish federally backed tribal government and to the domination of their reservation by non-Indian outsiders. Quickly, Native activists and supporters from across North America arrived to bolster their effort, but even more quickly Wounded Knee was surrounded by a counterforce consisting of tribal government police, U.S. Marshals, FBI agents, and Pentagon advisors, equipped with helicopters, armored personnel carriers, and lethal weapons. Roads into the village were blocked. There was a seventy-one-day siege, punctuated with frequent fire-fights in which many people were injured and two were killed.

Susan Jordan once again sat me down. "This is really important. You have to go and write about it," she said. "Yeah, but I just got home, and I'm broke." Susan took out her checkbook, and I was on my way.

• • •

The shooting was pretty much over by the time I got to South Dakota. (Here's me, once again, close to the action but at minimal personal risk. Some say there's no such thing as coincidence; I'm more inclined toward chaos theory.) People in Wounded Knee were weary and dispirited, the second person had just been killed, and negotiations were under way to end the two-month standoff. The several hundred occupiers, their guns notwithstanding, had set up a confrontation impossible to win. They were surrounded by an opponent with unlimited power. Supplies had to be snuck into the village on foot, at night, along the shallow draws that score that mostly treeless prairie like the creases in my sixty-eight-year-old face. They had declared themselves the Independent Oglala Nation. Their demands were righteous but verging on revolutionary: prose-cution, by the government, of civil rights violations perpetrated by that government; the honoring of long-disregarded treaty rights, which would have meant return of lands illegally transferred from the tribe over the course of a century; and the relinquishing of U.S. power on their territory. At a time when the jargon of revolution was everyday parlance, and small insurrections against behemoth power were idealized as a viable way to start one, Wounded Knee spoke vividly to a lot of people. And more so because it was a militant and moving stand by the most mistreated, and most easily romanticized, people among us.

I'm intrigued by the similarities and contrasts to the fight being led right now by the Standing Rock Sioux in North Dakota, against the Dakota Access Pipeline. The provenance is the same—ancestral lands, treaty rights, traditional culture versus assimilation. But the demand is specific, for cancelation of an infrastructure project that already has broad opposition because it would extend reliance on petroleum. The argument is that the pipeline will disturb sites sacred to the Sioux while posing an environmental threat to them and millions of other people. Over the months, thousands have arrived to participate, including members of more than two hundred Native tribes. Some are settling in, as I write, for the winter and a protracted battle; they've even set up a school that teaches kids both standard curriculum and Native languages and history. It's like Wounded Knee, only more focused, bigger in numbers— social media, unavailable in 1973, surely helps—but less grandiose. Also less reckless. The tactics are those of militant non-violence: people march, blockade highways, chain themselves to construction vehicles. Just this weekend, at least 127 were arrested doing so, and in a very of-the-moment moment, a camera-equipped drone that demonstrators were using to record confrontations was shot down by the cops. People are taking risks; the police have used dogs and mace on them. But it does seem possible that the goal might be achieved, and without loss of life. Maybe even without contributing to the everlasting cycle of escalation.

At Wounded Knee, of necessity in difficult circumstances, the photographers and print and radio journalists who arrived representing non-mainstream media pooled our resources. Radio news was broadcast over a smattering of college and community stations around the country—NPR's network was still in its infancy—and via technology that now seems quaint. The reporters spliced together clips from interviews with their commentaries, on magnetic tape, and transmitted these feeds via long-distance phone lines. They would unscrew the mouthpiece on a telephone handset, and use alligator clips to tap a pair of wires inside and connect the phone to a tape player. When the confrontation ended, their hundreds of hours of recordings, and the thousands of photographs and everybody's notes and experiences that had been amassed, seemed too valuable to put on a shelf. An offer to publish a book came from *Akwesasne Notes*, then the principal national newspaper of the North American Native world, based at the St. Regis Mohawk Reservation—Akwesasne, in Mohawk—in far Upstate New York.

With three others who had been at Wounded Knee I spent the fall and winter of '73–74, often snowed in, in a drafty old farmhouse down a dirt road fifty yards from the Quebec border. We transcribed, edited, typeset, photo-cropped, and pasted up *Voices from Wounded Knee* using pre-digital print technology as archaic as those alligator clips: an IBM Selectric typewriter, X-Acto knives, rubber cement. Once the book went to the printer, the other three moved on. I stayed at Akwesasne planning its distribution and promotion and working on the newspaper. I was there in all roughly a year.

Weatherpeople loved Wounded Knee for its military aspect, and, like others, were touched by the romance. Also, the Native American sovereignty movement seemed to fit perfectly into our Third-Worldist, anti-imperialist analysis. But I didn't have much contact with the underground that year. I was immersed in Native America. I didn't miss my old friends as I had in Chicago. There were people at Akwesasne who hoped I would stay on indefinitely; it was less than obliquely suggested that I might marry a Mohawk woman. I felt welcomed, as much as an outsider might be, but aware that this wasn't my world. Or where I might ever figure out my sexuality (the vaguer formulation I preferred rather than wondering bluntly whether I might ever come out). I could continue to write about Indian Country, but I knew I had to get myself to a city to get on with my life. I managed to arrange a contact with Jeff. Was there someplace I might go where I could be useful to—and a real part of—the organization? This time the answer was yes.

• • •

I had been making myself receptive to traditional Native American concepts about spirituality, about nature and its exploitation and humanity's place in it, even to the intimation that apparent facts on the ground such as the geopolitical reality of the United States of America might be transitory. Some of this involved unabashedly magical thinking. Meanwhile the Weather Underground had been moving in a roughly opposite direction. Maybe the leadership was embarrassed by the loose, stoned early underground days, or motivated by desperation at their own creeping irrelevance—the organization still did the occasional "symbolic" bombing of a restroom, but these were losing their wow factor. So in what would ultimately be revealed as the first piece of a strategy to exert control over the mass radical movement, the leaders had been busy writing a polemic in the time-tested Marxist vein, and restructuring the organization in the time-tested Leninist mode.

Time-tested and proven to fail—in my opinion now, and in my vague instincts then. But desperate self-aggrandizing people do stupid things. Including, in this case, taking a U-turn and adopting essentially what had been PL's politics and methods in 1969. The dominant focus would now be economic relationships and worker organizing—where before emphasis on race had distinguished us. It also meant adoption of what in communist newspeak is called "democratic centralism," a form of organization that in every instance where it has been applied turns out to be all centralism and no democracy. This may be a good way to run an army, and it also works more or less well as a way to run a totalitarian country. But by 1974 there was already ample evidence that it was a complete failure at producing societies anybody would actually want to live in.

Our leaders had long since stopped being called the Weather Bureau, referring to themselves after that, with feigned humility, simply as "our collective." Now they called themselves a Central Committee, under which a newly contrived and rigid hierarchy was instated. Relationships with aboveground people like me that had been imprecisely defined—and at least in my case, largely social—were being formalized. We would join, along with comrades who were underground, secret collectives with designated leaders and regular meetings. These groupings would be dedicated to the politics expressed in the Central Committee's lofty forth-coming analysis of the world, a book called *Prairie Fire*, and to carrying out the program of what was now calling itself, just slightly pompously, the Weather Underground Organization (WUO). I belittle the grandiosity and the mind-numbing lack of originality of all this, you will notice, but I went along with it then, moving to Boston and joining one of those cells.

The writing of *Prairie Fire* was represented as an open process, and while many people, both members and supporters, were asked to comment on its draft, it had a narrow and unyielding ideology. This could have been articulated in 1969—and more or less had been by our old enemy Progressive Labor, not that the ideas were original to them. For that matter it could have dated from 1939, or maybe 1889. Fine-tuning of the document was welcome, but disagreement was ignored or perceived as an assault. It would be too migraine-inducing to critique the whole thing now; besides, it's long since been tossed onto the dung heap of history. But *Prairie Fire*'s treatment of sexual politics will serve as an illustration of its strained superficiality.

It described the exploitation of women as a function of capitalism, neglecting to mention the institution of patriarchy. Regarding sexuality itself, the document acknowledged that unequal power between women and men limits intimacy. It called lesbianism a response that helps create unity among women, and asserted the right of people to their sexual preferences. But the authors could not bring themselves to explicitly mention gay men at all, other than to gratuitously say that "not all gay culture transcends the sexism of U.S. life." (There are pages and pages of analysis of race but no similarly snarky line amounting to "not all black culture is free of the influence of racism.")

The considerable body of contemporary feminist theory that existed by 1974 was ignored, although the women's movement was praised for having produced changes in mass consciousness. But these were described rather too sweepingly, like, you know, prairie fires that have already burned the landscape clean. "The overthrowing of rotten values of male supremacy...was a wonderful advance," and, "Men, too, are understanding that sexism makes them emotionally barren and culturally warped." One of my first tasks on moving to Boston was to show the draft to a few old friends of the organization who, out of nostalgia and hope, I imagine, had not yet totally rejected us—the way you don't necessarily cut loose a friend who's been acting crazy. One of them was Marge Piercy. Her response to the document's treatment of sexual politics, in particular, was incredulity. "What country are these people living in, anyway?" she demanded to know.

I wasn't clear or brave enough to take on the document's sexual politics. But I did comment from the perspective I had been absorbing from reading books like *Small Is Beautiful* and *The Population Bomb*, which may no longer be particularly apt responses to the challenges of sustainability but at least were addressing them, and from ideas I'd encountered in Indian Country, where contrary to the magical thinking of some on the left Indian people did not see themselves as participants in any leftist revolution at all. Jeff was delegated to deliver the Central Committee's response to me, because I was his problem, I guess.

The encounter started off like so many others: the big hug, the drive to a pretty spot, the long walk around a lake. But his task was, as we used to say, to smash. "You took a position against cities," he said—vastly overstating what I had written, which hadn't been a position at all but a series of questions—"and against industry. We're talking about a socialist revolution, like Russia, like China. Factories. Workers. Within the U.S. borders as we know them. That's what it's about, and you're wrong." Jeff did not seem to be enjoying himself. I sure wasn't. How could I have enjoyed submitting to people who rejected what I had to say? Still, I caved, and mumbled some retraction. That was the price of remaining in the organization. And I wanted to be in the organization, so it didn't occur to me to wonder, if my ideas were so out of line, why the organization would still want me. At the least, this relationship was, in the term being popularized at the time, co-dependent. From the vantage point of today, I could say it resembled an abusive marriage. Even then, I might have remembered that my choices to be part of all this were mainly driven by friendship and community. This didn't feel like friendship. But I couldn't face the alternative, taking responsibility for my own life, that thing you can only do by yourself. Which is to say, I couldn't face growing up.

• • •

I was delighted to learn that among the members of my Boston collective would be Karin Ashley and Phoebe Hirsch, both close friends in my earliest SDS days whom I hadn't seen for a long time. But during the next two years, while we met every week or two, I had not a single visit with either of them simply as a friend. I never saw Jeff, or Mike, or anyone else from the underground who was not in our cell. My visits to the forest were no longer several-day stays, or strolls in a park; there were no more campfires, real or metaphorical.

Instead I would make a tedious series of bus and subway connections across the city, and then walk along a specified route, being observed to make sure I wasn't followed. Once we'd assembled in this way, we would spend an afternoon uncomfortably huddled in some too-public place—a corner of a college library, typically, pretending to be studying together for an exam. Actually we might really be studying—something vitally relevant such as Joseph Stalin's 1913 disquisition *Marxism and the National Question*—or perhaps we were being force-fed the latest directive from the Central Committee. If the organization had been too relaxed and social before, we were making up for it with coldly impersonal, machine-like industry now—Weather Machine 2.0. "A revolution is not a dinner party," Mao Tse-Tung had famously written. But was there some principled reason why we couldn't at least have tea and cookies, and a little gossip?

Prairie Fire was printed clandestinely, and deposited as if by magic on the doorsteps of radical activists and organizations in the small hours of a single summer morning in 1974. Like other members of the WUO, I enlisted a couple of sympathizers to make some of these drops. Then it was the job of members like me who were not underground to make sure the treatise was spread around and discussed among activists. This document may not be perfect, we were instructed to say, but it's like a gift, so much great thinking, let's use it as a framework for dialogue. We announced the formation of a Prairie Fire Distributing Committee, to reprint the book and circulate it widely. In Boston we had a series of informal gatherings—a picnic on the banks of the Charles River, intimate brunches in people's kitchens, even a weekend retreat at a farmhouse in the New Hampshire countryside—where there was lively conversation and amicable debate. Organizing these get-togethers, I somehow managed to still believe that the book had been offered genuinely, as a means of engagement.

The aboveground members of my collective included Laura Whitehorn, whom I had known glancingly during the Machine days in Chicago. Laura had relentless energy and a lightning-fast, impregnable opinion about everything. Perhaps in reward for these qualities she was designated as one of our two leaders, along with a Central Committee member who was based in Boston. It was by Laura that the hidden agenda was revealed to me. It turned out that the distributing committee wasn't formed simply to pass the book around. We would soon change its name to Prairie Fire Organizing Committee (PFOC). The PFOC would serve as a front group through which the WUO could use its aboveground members to operate within and influence the mass movement. (If you don't know the jargon of the Marxist-Leninist left, be advised that an "organizing committee" is synonymous with, or meant to lead to, a "pre-party formation," which is a highfalutin self-description for a grouplet that wants to be the nucleus of a new communist party and hence the revolutionary vanguard. The addition of "organization" to the name Weather Underground had the same connotation.)

I objected to this strategy as manipulative and bound to arouse suspicion—and also impractical, because almost all of the people we'd been having conversations with about *Prairie Fire* were already doing organizing work and were unlikely to subordinate that to whatever we proposed, or to willingly add another schedule of meetings to their calendars. Objection overruled. "This is the plan," Laura declared. A disciplined communist now, I helped carry it out.

As it happened, only about eight or ten people joined with us secret weather operatives in the PFOC's Boston group. This scenario was replicated in a handful of other cities. In the summer of 1975, these PFOC groups all gathered in Boston. We declared ourselves a national organization with allegiance to the politics of *Prairie Fire.* There were, I believe, six chapters and a total membership of seventy-five, maybe a hundred. At this Boston conference, we WUO plants also promulgated a plan for a big gathering of leftist and grassroots activists, the National Hard Times Conference, to be held in the coming winter. In all this, functioning like an alien space invader through the bodies of people like me, was the invisible force of the WUO and its Central Committee, hoping to recapture its lost standing atop the mass movement.

• • •

Invisible—though it must have been laughably obvious to anybody who was paying attention that the WUO and the PFOC were umbilically connected. We certainly didn't fool the cops, as their dossiers reveal. And surely there were people in the movement who assumed that anyone like me or Laura, known to have been in Weatherman in 1969 and now eagerly promoting the organization's manifesto and grand scheme, must be part of it still. But I think a lot of people chose not to know, or not to say anything indicating their hunches, for the same reasons that some people continued to support the organization in material ways, even if they had misgivings. People in the left wanted to protect the underground because it had successfully hidden itself for so long, which counted as a victory for our (weak) side and an embarrassment for the (strong) government. People not only romanticized but also genuinely respected the boldness and risk-taking, and certainly didn't want to do or say anything that could lead to fugitives being captured. But by the *Prairie Fire* period, to protect the WUO was in effect to encourage a devious cabal who were not particularly interested in hearing your ideas but definitely wanted to tell you what to do.

Nowadays, the concept of a righteous underground owes a lot to the Underground Railroad. Most people's awareness of that history is relatively recent but even without it, for my generation, clandestine action presented itself as an honorable way to subvert evil. For people of my background growing up before African American history was widely articulated and honored, the idea of an underground derived more from the anti-Nazi resistance in World War II. You hid the Jew in your crawl space because it was the right thing to do. You hustled the downed British flyer out of the country, or sabotaged the railroad trestle, because those were right actions in a battle against unquestionable evil. And then there was the less sober but still subversive idea in the air during my youth, of a cultural underground encompassing protest music, illegal drugs, communal living, and the rejection of conventional ideas about careers, money, sex, dress, manners, and just about everything else. All that was also referred to, at the time, as "underground."

"I see your point about Weather having contributed to a culture of violence. But they were not pioneers," the historian Art Eckstein commented to me in an email. (His book *Bad Moon Rising: How the Weather Underground Beat the FBI and Lost the Revolution* is intensively researched and richly detailed, and manages to be both empathetic and critical.) Against the long list of bombings by leftists, anarchists, and other persons that predated and coincided with ours, Art thought that our contribution to the culture of violence was relatively minor, but noted that most of those other actions have been forgotten. He wondered, "So why is Weather famous? Why does Weather remain famous?"

I see lots of reasons why. We arose at a peak moment of mass activism and militance, atop the highly visible platform of SDS. We were children of television and the advertising age, and instinctively knew how to play to the media. Other armed groups of the day mostly styled themselves armies—the Black Liberation Army, the Symbionese Liberation Army. In a particularly media-savvy if accidental stroke of brilliance, we actually incorporated the word underground into our name. It conjures up an altogether different image, less fearsomely militaristic, more intimate and saintly. Picture the sage old woman in the remote farmhouse who risks her own safety by giving the hunted fugitives a bed and a delicious bowl of stew. The relative restraint of our actions plus the noble-outlaw imagery rendered us warm and fuzzy, revolutionaries you would want to cuddle up with. As to what continues to fuel the persistence of interest in Weatherman, or Weather mythology: the vast majority of us did not die or end up in prison for life, so have been available for interviews by journalists and historians; the privileged-white-kids-in-revolt theme has been irresistible to novelists and filmmakers; and quite a few of us have published our own versions of the story. Mine will probably contribute to our outsized importance, too, though I mean to dispel some of the myths.

But why did people still actively provide support to the WUO in 1976? For some the motivation was simple loyalty and concern for friends whose obnoxious or wrongheaded ideas and actions were beside the point. During that year I spent on the SDS staff in Washington, I had a part-time job in the mail room of a non-profit concerned with housing the poor, where I made friends with Barbara Leckie, an art student who was working there as a secretary. She came from a leftist family, in fact was named after her parents' friend Barbara Deming, a prominent feminist, civil rights, and antiwar writer and leader with a deep commitment to non-violence. During all the underground years, I stayed in touch with Barbara Leckie, but kept her separate from my public life. She would write to me at a mail drop. Sometimes to ensure that I wasn't being tracked on my way to a visit in the forest I would spend a day or two with her in Baltimore, where she had moved. So she understood that she was supporting my connection with the organization. Recently she found and gave me all the letters I sent her in those years. Reading them, I am mortified to see that I was constantly spouting the Weather balderdash du jour, at excruciating length, and urging her to read various tomes that were in vogue with us. As if Barbara Leckie needed political education from the likes of me. One of the earliest of these letters was written on N.O. stationery a month before the Days of Rage, when Weatherman was intent on isolating ourselves; she and I had just briefly seen each other. I wrote, "I am more and more finding that living and working the way we do makes it a real trip to spend time with people who are not directly & immediately involved in one's scene." Barbara's comment now: "What I thought then, given my background as a red diaper baby, was that if you (all) were trying to foment a revolution, you had a rough road to hoe if I was a challenge." I only have my side of our correspondence, but I'm pretty sure she never rushed out to buy the books I urged on her, or responded at any length to my ravings, but simply carried on caring for me as a person, politics aside. Reading my letters to her makes me squirm, but I do like seeing what nice handwriting I used to have. Nowadays I find my own scrawl nearly illegible.

• • •

I'm generally pessimistic about the future of humanity and the planet, but I was feeling slightly hopeful about the situation in North Dakota. Until what happened yesterday, October 27, 2016. It's hard enough to know what really occurs in a confrontation when you're present, and harder from a distance. But some or all of this apparently took place: Law enforcement bulldozed an encampment, using pepper spray and rubber bullets on protesters. A loose-cannon security guard in the employ of the pipeline company arrived waving an assault rifle; he, or somebody, was shot and his company truck torched. One or more protesters fired guns at police, but didn't hit any. Protesters burned hay bales and tires, and tossed firebombs. Police arrested 141 people.

Does a belief in the efficacy of militant non-violence amount to magical thinking? Non-violence was a critical component of the civil rights movement, as long as demonstrators were willing to let themselves be beaten up and get busted. Then some people concluded that change wasn't coming fast enough, or that the demands weren't sweeping enough, or that they couldn't submit to such mistreatment. Thus we had the Black Panthers and other armed liberation groups—and Weatherman. I had assumed that people going to Standing Rock had left their guns at home and would not be mixing up Molotov cocktails. Naïve me. Why, after all, given the ample evidence of history, should they trust law enforcement—its officials, or its loose-cannon hired guns—to refrain from violence, and so why abstain from violence themselves?

So is escalation inevitable? Decades after I had last seen him on that snowy day on the wharf in St. John, New Brunswick, I crossed paths again with Mark Rudd. His big, blustery personality hadn't changed; personalities don't. He can still use up all the oxygen in a room, but he has also become reflective, self-critical about his role in the early leadership of Weatherman, and a vocal advocate of pacifism. He calls pacifism the only morally defensible stance, though he concedes, "I know it's totally impractical." In the Sixties, I was glad anytime the pacifists in the movement drenched draft board files with blood or otherwise gummed up the works, and I appreciated pacifists for going to jail or on hunger strikes because their suffering and witness put the government to shame. But mostly I was contemptuous of them. The moral impulse that had propelled me to join that decorous picket line at thirteen had been overwhelmed by anger. When I met Barbara Leckie, I thought it was cool that she was named after a famous activist, but I never read anything Barbara Deming wrote. Now I see that among Deming's most-referenced essays is one called "On Revolution and Equilibrium." The title alone makes my head spin. The concepts of revolution and equilibrium together comprise a koan—a puzzle, a provocation, something to meditate on in hopes of enlightenment. Is the interpenetration of revolution and equilibrium even a possibility?

• • •

I was one of the "secret" WUO operatives facilitating the PFOC and National Hard Times Conference strategy—or better put, plot—roughly from mid-1974 until mid-1976. This was the bleakest period in my life, because it was the most dishonest. I was ambivalent about *Prairie Fire* and disliked the organizing strategy that came with it. Our politics had been wrongheaded during the earlier phases of Weatherman, too, but then at least I believed wholeheartedly. That made it seem as if I had agency. It made being in the organization thrilling. But this was denial and hollowness and fakery.

Because the scheme arose from the WUO's desire to connect with and influence the mass movement, we in PFOC were driven to conduct "mass work." Our efforts were ungrounded and mostly fruitless. There was a lot of leafleting at subway stops during rush hour. It was decided that I should take a few classes at a community college, so that I could meet working class young people and attempt to enlist them. I of course was not a working class person, I was not there as the typical students were, to learn anything that would help me find employment (although I did acquire some useful basic Spanish), and I had very little else in common with them. It was an entirely artificial situation.

Boston in those years was convulsed by the violent resistance of white communities to a federal court order to integrate the public schools through busing. PFOC attempted to insert ourselves into this conflict by mounting a weekly picket line at the office of the Boston School Committee. None of us happened to have children who attended the Boston public schools, or any children at all, and most of us lived in Cambridge and Somerville, not Boston.

Everybody has the right to object to instances of blatant racism, regardless of where they live, but we were hardly well situated to play a useful role in this conflict, or to build real relationships with the people directly involved. We weren't building relationships with people who were already active on the left, either. The pretense of openness in those early conversations prompted by the publication of *Prairie Fire* vanished as we insisted on the rightness of the document and our activities, and rejected criticism. So even relationships—and friendships—we already had became brittle.

I had left Akwesasne in order to make a life—to settle, to write, to find a partner or at least address my sexual confusion. Also I had come to Boston to be a member, in the new structured mode, of the WUO. I was doing the latter, but not much the former. I had a job in a book warehouse for a while, and then collected unemployment until that ran out, and then was broke. Months behind on rent, I abandoned an apartment and moved into Laura's spare room, where I had no shelter from her relentless insistence that we be seen and heard everywhere at all times with our bullhorns and leaflets. I wasn't writing at all. One reason I had been glad to come to Boston was that I already had several friends there, and in my first months there, before the forced march of the PFOC got fully under way, through them I met more people—a community I could have become enmeshed in. But now my world had shrunk to consist only of comrades, and even with those who had once been real friends there was little experience of friendship. I had a couple of dates in this period with guys, hookups really, but without time or money or private space—or more important than those limitations, without taking control of my own life—none of these connections went anywhere. I even let Laura engineer a doomed relationship between me and a woman in the PFOC whom she was grooming for recruitment into the WUO. I was ill a lot with vague ailments that I can see now were caused by stress. I was ignoring my needs emotionally and physically, and in denial about the politics, too.

The Vietnam War was ending, and with it went the primary source of mass radical sentiment. The country was in recession then. The National Hard Times Conference was put forward as a venue for reinventing and coordinating a mass movement centered on working class economic demands. The WUO conceived it and the PFOC called for it, and it was we worker bees of PFOC who actually made it happen. We made a point of soliciting other organizations, especially non-white ones, to endorse the idea and to people a steering committee. Activists genuinely wanted to connect and find commonality, so much so that two thousand people from all over the country and many different organizations and communities were willing to come to Chicago over a frigid February weekend in 1976 to attend.

It had been consciousness, fanaticism even, about race that had set Weatherman apart from much of the left in 1969: racism as the organizing principle of American society, white people's privilege as the impediment to their solidarity with people of color. Today, given the acute awareness of racially tilted phenomena like police killings and incarceration rates, this knowledge is much more widely accepted among white people. At the time, even many on the left ignored it. But now came the ultimate perversion of that original core of our politics. It would be race, our own racism, that rendered the National Hard Times Conference a failure. And with that failure would begin the unraveling of the Weather Underground Organization itself. The PFOC came to the conference with a political platform, written for us by the Central Committee of the WUO of course, to ram through. This was a "Hard Times Bill of Rights," an uninspired list of old-fashioned socialist demands. We also came with an action program to propose, centered on attending the upcoming counter-Bicentennial march in Philadelphia on July 4 of that year. You heard me right: Come to a national conference in February, so you can come to a national demonstration in July! That's what we had to offer.

Most people who attended the conference wanted to network and learn from each other about their actual circumstances and organizing projects. No doubt some of that went on, but it wasn't our concern. I, for example, who had convinced some Indian leaders I knew to come to Chicago, am described—mortifyingly—in the report of an FBI informant as haranguing the Native American workshop about the imperative of socialist revolution. Was I specifically ordered to do this or was it my own lobotomized initiative? "The Indians in attendance at this workshop all advised," the police observer had no trouble perceiving, "that they are not interested in...any other causes, other than their own interest in obtaining sovereignty." I also had convinced two kids from the community college to attend the conference. Maybe they learned something, and took up some constructive political work, and if so maybe the time I spent hanging around that campus wasn't a total waste. But I don't remember their names and never even saw them again, which says all you need to know about the depth of the relationships I had built with them.

The conference started off badly, with Jennifer Dohrn, representing the PFOC, giving an embarrassingly inarticulate keynote address on Friday night. By the Sunday afternoon closing plenary session, when we meant to have our platform and program accepted by a vote, there began a ripple, and then an avalanche, of criticism. People had gone to a lot of trouble to come, responding to the conference's call in hopeful good faith. They found themselves confronting a surreptitious but palpably operative controlling faction that was trying to shove its proposals down everybody else's throats. Our manipulation was not the only thing that bothered them. It was not lost on this multi-racial gathering that the source of the fixed agenda was the all-white PFOC. You guys, people said out loud in just these words, are a bunch of racists. That's what we ought to talk about, not your Hard Times Bill of Rights. The conference ended in a mood of rancor and alienation.

The morning after this debacle, there was a meeting of the shell-shocked PFOC. Members who were not secret WUO functionaries began to question where these failed ideas had been emanating from. The PFOC leadership, which is to say those of us who were WUO plants, for the first time had no glib response prepared because it hadn't occurred to us that the conference could blow up in our faces, and we hadn't yet met with our handlers to devise a strategy for damage control. Even once we had, the questioning within the PFOC could not be stopped. A pattern people had perhaps only sensed, or had pretended wasn't there, had become visible, and could not be hidden again. The resentment grew. Within a few months it had been formalized as a "rectification campaign" of criticism and required self-criticism, of overthrowing leadership, of excruciating revisions of dogmatic arcana. Some who had been in the duplicitous situation of secret WUO membership confessed and recanted, and named others of us as their co-conspirators. Leaders were deposed and new leaders self-declared. It was a scoundrel time of show trials, pageants of accusation, and guilt.

"Rectification" reached its accusing finger deep within the bowels of the underground itself. The denunciations and mea culpas, the rationalizations and fallback positions circled vertiginously. One group put forward an argument for "inversion," saying that the whole underground enterprise had hampered the mass movement by keeping so many skilled organizers in limbo; everyone should surface, turn themselves in, deal with their legal problems, and become public activists again. But another faction accused the first of renouncing the sacred clandestine struggle. It reached a degree of insanity in the underground itself, I have been told, where people whose self-criticisms and self-reinventions were not deemed sufficient or correct were seen as therefore functioning "objectively" as cops, and so all the resources they had ever known about—every car, apartment, name on a set of ID, even the secret print shop that had been assembled at enormous expense and caution to publish *Prairie Fire* and other propaganda—were simply abandoned. But I cannot furnish many details about the organization's disintegration. It went on for quite some time, I understand. But I had no stomach for it. By summer, I knew that for me, it was over.

My original impulse as an activist had been innocent and idealistic. I wanted to humanize the world. This thing I had helped create was now a grotesque caricature. It took years for me to unravel my whole experience in Weatherman. But I was acutely aware at the time that I hadn't liked the retrograde politics of *Prairie Fire* or approved of the duplicitous PFOC strategy. I had gone along and was ashamed of doing so, but I wasn't about to repent for it now before the martinets who had just seized power from the earlier bunch of blockheads. I was twenty-eight years old. I was finally ready to take responsibility for my own life.

I was angry, at myself most of all, and exhausted, as if I'd just willingly spent seven years married to a manipulative psychopath when I could have escaped him any time. I went around in tears, in a kind of mourning. It wasn't entirely easy to quit. Jennifer made a trip to Boston from New York to try to talk me into denouncing myself so that I could have a place in the new order. Laura presented me with an invoice, for debts I didn't know I was accruing while living in her apartment. Then I was given a chance to see Jeff. Maybe it was thought that a taste of revenge would be addictive and bring me back into the venomous fold. He looked gray and deflated. "How could you not listen to your own people? Why would you not listen to me?" I asked. Possibly he was expecting the sort of indictment, framed in tortured Marxist-Leninist ideological jargon, that others were subjecting him to. If so, he had forgotten who I was. I would have liked an apology, some acknowledgment that our friendship had been violated or at least neglected, some expression of regret. Any emotion at all, in fact. He just shrugged, and dissembled. We parted on the street. I didn't look back.

Now

Four decades have passed. Today is November 7, 2016.

President Obama suggested last week that perhaps the route of the Dakota Access Pipeline might be changed, in response to the protests, to protect sacred lands. Still, out there on the prairie, the conflict seems to be escalating. Then on NPR, a protester described a gentle new tactic they are using. They hold mirrors up in front of the cops and ask them to "look at themselves, and look at us," she explained, "and see that the only weapon we have is prayer." Reflection, in either of its senses, can indeed be a kind of prayer: look deeply at yourself, look deeply within. Perhaps, on the brink of confrontation, this gesture can inspire moments of pause and equilibrium, even connection between opponents. But some on the scene in North Dakota possess weapons other than prayer. Law enforcement does; some protesters surely do as well. It won't surprise me if the next thing I hear from out there is that people have been killed.

Tomorrow is the Presidential election, about which all possible nightmare superlatives have been used to death. This morning I am online, trying to trade my safe New York Hillary Clinton vote for the principled but throwaway third-party protest vote of someone in a swing state. This would represent an unconventional form of engagement with conventional politics, a tiny act of perfectly legal manipulation in hopes of delaying the chaos that awaits, if only for another few years. Gaming the system? No, just participating, working a compromise, which is the way the system is supposed to work.

So it has come to this: The would-be bomb thrower will visit his polling place, chat amiably with his neighbors, take his paper ballot and darken the small circles completely. He will make no stray marks.

In 1968 I shouted that "the elections don't mean shit" and led people off the sidewalks to "vote in the streets." I was a member of an avowed revolutionary underground until eight years after that. But actually I have voted in every election, everywhere I have lived, since 1972 when the antiwar presidential candidate George McGovern lost miserably to Richard Nixon. Since I walked away from the WUO, though, I have not been a political activist in any traditional sense, either of the radical or mainstream variety. Just picturing life within an organization makes me feel short of breath. I've had enough of organization for a lifetime. Instead I have been contributing to society in a largely solitary way, by writing. I mostly focus on topics I care and have a point of view about—environment, urban planning, how cities intersect with their surroundings. Even when writing about things that lack that urgency—travel, dining, interior design—and in writing novels, I believe that I am adding to the general level of literacy and thoughtfulness in our increasingly illiterate and thoughtless culture. This has been enough.

But Peter and I both became involved in politics recently, at the hyperlocal scale of our very small city, where 6,500 people live in 2.5 square miles. I chair the Conservation Advisory Council. Its tasks include, for example, enhancing our quality of life through planting street trees and protecting open spaces, and preparing our Hudson River waterfront for higher tides and more frequent floods. Peter, born in 1959 so too young to have been a Sixties activist, is a leader in an effort to equalize our city's voting districts. Right now we are the only one in the United States that, instead of adjusting district boundaries every decade to reflect population shifts, gives the districts' representatives unequally weighted votes in city council. This keeps a backward-looking and venal clique in power. Attempts to change it have repeatedly been torpedoed by those with the weightier votes. In desperation, Peter and his co-conspirators made a plan. They drew a new district map, drafted a petition to force a referendum, and organized a sophisticated media campaign—all in perfect clandestinity. The initiative went public with a splashy launch that shocked the old guard. Dogged canvassing in the months since makes the proposition look like a winner. An enormous amount of this work has been done by Peter himself, who has the vision and diplomatic skills both to keep his comrades focused, and to cold-call strangers or engage them on the street. I understand what's involved, though I wouldn't have the patience. But I have enormously enjoyed the irony that while I am now a sworn official of the city, working within the system, my husband likes to joke that he is busy overthrowing the government.

Such modest efforts regarding quality of life, adaptation to climate change, and political equity might be successes in the near term. I fear that in the long run they won't make much difference. I expect that most of humanity is going to drown or die of thirst, or whatever, soon enough, regardless of how we try now to save the planet. I don't have much faith in the future of American democracy either, no matter which candidates and ballot initiatives are victorious tomorrow. Does civilization even have a prayer? Still, these tangible, local, and, in the global scheme of things, tiny acts we undertake keep us connected. That's not nothing. And they keep us conscious, which is better than going numb or crazy in terror of the future—even if they might not affect that future much. These are scary times. But now I understand that there has never been a time that wasn't.

John Mungo at the March on Washington for Lesbian, Gay and Bi Equal Rights and Liberation, April 25, 1993.

Photo by Jonathan Lerner.

Gratitude

The title of this book is adapted from a line of Bob Dylan's "A Hard Rain's A-Gonna Fall."

John Oakes prompted me to tell this story, when I thought I had long since uttered my last word on the Weathermen. I am grateful for his deep confidence in me, and for the chance he offered me to revisit this history and share it. Michael Alvear, Janet Axelrod, Art Eckstein, Eli Plenk, Janet Rosen, and Mike Spiegel read my first draft and offered invaluable criticism. My husband Peter Frank's enthusiasm and belief in this project allowed me to devote the time and space it required; I could not have done it without his love and support.

This book is dedicated to the memory of my psychotherapist John Wiley Mungo, who always gleefully referred to my Sixties as those days when I was "a big bad radical hippie."

JONATHAN LERNER dropped out of Antioch College and became a full-time activist on the staff of Students for a Democratic Society, the principle organization of the New Left. He was a founding member of the militant Weatherman faction, which took over SDS in 1969, and editor of its newspaper *Fire!*. He remained a member of the Weather Underground, while it carried out a campaign of bombings, until its demise in 1976. He is the author of the novels *Caught in a Still Place* and *Alex Underground*, and a journalist focusing on architectural, urbanist and environmental issues. He now lives in New York's Hudson Valley.